SANCTUARY

SANCTUARY

CHIEKO N. OKAZAKI

Deseret Book Company
Salt Lake City, Utah

Library of Congress Cataloging-in-Publication Data

Okazaki, Chieko N., 1926–
    Sanctuary / by Chieko N. Okazaki.
        p.   cm.
    Includes bibliographical references and index.
    ISBN 1-57345-154-1 (hardcover)
    1. Christian life—Mormon authors. I. Title.
BX8656.046   1997
248.4'89332—dc21   97-3488
                                                               CIP

Printed in the United States of America

10 9   8   7   6   5   4   3   2   1   72082

To my grandsons,
Matthew, Andrew, and William

CONTENTS

1

SANCTUARY

A sanctuary is a holy place, a place hallowed to God, a place of safety and refuge. In these times of stress, of menace, and of danger, what is our sanctuary? Where can we find sanctuary?

I have particular interest in the concept of sanctuary because these last few years have seemed to be years of such turmoil and stress for me. Each March is the anniversary of the death of my husband, Ed. My son and daughter-in-law experienced the sorrow of losing a child in death just a few days before he was due to be born. My brother underwent surgery for a cranial tumor. My mother had an operation for a hip replacement. My sister-in-law died of cancer of the pancreas, and my daughter-in-law's mother died of a very fast-acting cancer.

You can see why, in the changes and turmoil of my life, the hope of finding a sanctuary of peace and safety is such a power-ful one. Nor do I think I am the only one who is struggling with heavy burdens. Looking at women in church, well-dressed and clean, sitting in a beautiful setting, I'm sure many would think, "Oh, Mormon women are a privileged group, free of sorrow, stress, and burdens." I know better. In almost every group are those who are surviving the ongoing pain of divorce, of wasted potential, of faltering faith, of bearing the wounds of a beloved child or sibling who has used his or her agency to make terrible choices that have brought great suffering. In your family, or in the family of someone close to you, is someone working through the difficult realizations of chronic physical illness, of mental or emotional instability, of physical or sexual abuse, of same-sex attraction, of chemical dependency, of injustice done to you or a loved one, of sorrow, of loneliness, of discouragement. All of us have moments, at least—and for some of us those moments stretch into years—when we are heart-hungry for the feeling of sanctuary. Where can it be found?

I'm sure that many of us immediately think of the peace and serenity we find in the temple when we are experiencing true communion with the Lord. Or perhaps we think of home as the place where we want most to be in times of trouble, of how nurtured and loved we feel there, and how we want to provide peace and protection for our children. Sanctuary can be found in thoughts of a beloved friend or parent or sibling or spouse—someone who knows our heart and accepts us completely. And, of course, we associate the concept of sanctuary with the boundless love of God for all of us.

Let me share with you a story that combines several concepts of sanctuary: the family, the temple, and the love of God. Larry Barkdull's mother, a painter, resolved to "paint her testimony"—a painting of Jesus praying in Gethsemane—as the fullest expression of her belief. She spent many hours working on her painting, and when it was finished, it was hung outside the celestial room of the Idaho Falls Temple. But Larry's mother did not see it there. There was a divorce, followed by health problems that ended in her addiction to pain-relieving drugs, and poverty. During the time that her children were marrying, she had to wait outside the temple, but she never lost her testimony, and she never gave up working to regain control of her life. She raised her family, conquered her addictions, gave volunteer service to handicapped children, and worked with recovering substance abusers. She married a good man civilly, returned to the temple where she was able to see her painting on its wall for the first time, was sealed to her husband a year later, and within six months was dead of pancreatic and liver cancer. The painting was returned to the family some time later, and hanging it in Larry's family room was an emotional high point for the family as he told the grandchildren of their grandmother's struggles to "stay true to her church and her God."[1]

For Doris Barkdull, the sanctuary of her home was broken by divorce, and the consequent complications of the divorce and substance abuse prevented her from entering the temple for many years. But in the sanctuary of her heart, her testimony remained strong.

Let's think about sanctuaries, all kinds of places of refuge where we may seek the Spirit of the Lord. In the scriptures, most mentions of the word *sanctuary* refer to a specific place, the tabernacle or temple. Consider this Old Testament passage about *the* sanctuary, meaning the portable tabernacle that God instructed the children of Israel to build as part of their reorientation toward him in the wilderness.

> And the Lord spake unto Moses, saying,
>
> Speak unto the children of Israel, that they bring me an offering: of every man that giveth it willingly with his heart ye shall take my offering.
>
> And this is the offering which ye shall take of them; gold, and silver, and brass,
>
> And blue, and purple, and scarlet, and fine linen, and goats' hair,
>
> And rams' skins dyed red, and badgers' skins, and . . . spices for anointing oil. . . .
>
> And let them make me a sanctuary; that I may dwell among them. (Exodus 25:1–8)

These are specific instructions involving many different fabrics, textures, and colors, but the point is obviously not the interior-decorating scheme but the last verse: God will dwell among his people if they will make a sanctuary for him. Does God need a sanctuary, a place where he can be protected and shielded? No, but he needs a place where he can be regarded with reverence and awe. He needs, in other words, a people who recognize holiness.

In turn, he can provide sanctuary for them. We read in Isaiah: "Sanctify the Lord of hosts himself . . . and he shall be for a sanctuary" (Isaiah 8:13–14). Similarly, the Lord promised, regarding the children of Israel, "Although I have cast them far off among the heathen, and among the countries, yet will I be to them as a little sanctuary in the countries where they shall come" (Ezekiel 11:16).

Then in the New Testament, the concept of sanctuary becomes an integral part of our understanding of the covenant of redemption:

> We have such [a] high priest, who is set on the right hand of the throne of the Majesty in the heavens;
>
> A minister of the sanctuary, and of the true tabernacle, which the Lord pitched, and not man. . . .
>
> Seeing then that we have a great high priest, that is passed into the heavens, Jesus the Son of God, let us hold fast our profession.
>
> For we have not an high priest which cannot be touched with the feeling of our infirmities; but was in all points tempted like as we are, yet without sin.
>
> Let us therefore come boldly unto the throne of grace, that we may obtain mercy, and find grace to help in time of need. (Hebrews 8:1–2; 4:14–16)

Our temples and our homes are physical structures, but it is the spirit within them that is important, not the shapes and colors they happen to have. President Thomas S. Monson stressed this spiritual aspect of sanctuary when he described happy homes: "Happy homes come in a variety of appearances. Some feature large families with father, mother, brothers, and sisters living together in a spirit of love. Others consist of a single parent with one or two children, while other homes have but one occupant." He described a motto that his aunt had embroidered and hung on the wall of his grandmother's house: "Choose your love; love your choice."[2]

"Home" and "family," according to Elder L. Tom Perry, "must be interpreted to encompass the lives of the single Latter-day Saint, single LDS parents and their children, and married Saints who have no children."[3]

The important point is that there is not only one right way to create a home or to be a family. Therefore, there is not just one right way to make a sanctuary of your home. Think about your own home, the people who live there, and the activities that occur. Perhaps yours is a lively place of scarlet and purple, and the ram's wool may still be on your little lambs, and they may have just charged through the family room at top speed for the third time in five minutes. That's all right. Is there love? Is there holiness? Is there the happiness that betokens the Spirit of the Lord?

Sometimes we think that we have to be sitting quietly in a meeting or engaged in prayer to feel the Spirit, and that reverence is the same thing as immobility. Not a bit of it! Look for signs of love and happiness as well as reverence and peace, and you'll find the Spirit of the Lord in them as well.

A sanctuary isn't a fortress that bars people from entering it, and it's not a mausoleum where everything is hushed and still. It's a place of holiness, a place of happiness, and a place of love. Your children, your friends, and your neighbors will be able to feel if your home offers a sanctuary.

I think it's interesting that the Old Testament also describes cities of refuge where someone who had accidentally killed another could flee from vengeance and live until the death of the reigning high priest. Then the old blood feuds were canceled and the slayer could return home without fear of vengeance (see Numbers 35).

The children of Israel no longer had cities of refuge in New Testament times, but I was interested to read in the Doctrine and Covenants that Zion would serve such a purpose: "And it shall be called the New Jerusalem, a land of peace, a city of refuge, a place of safety for the saints of the Most High God" (D&C 45:66). We know that the stakes of Zion are the places of gathering for the Saints today. Isn't it wonderful to think of every ward and every stake as a place of refuge and a place of safety for the Saints? It is a marvelous ideal to hold up.

Another sanctuary I think we all need in our troubled world is the feeling that there is another person or another group of people with whom we can be safe. For us as women, I hope that we can find a sanctuary of sisterhood in the Relief Society. I hope Relief Society will be a place of acceptance and trust, a place of listening and sharing, a place of comfort and strength. And I hope that many strong relationships will flourish as friendships, in little groups of two or three where the trust in that relationship is considered sacred and where the privilege of ministering to each other's needs is holy.

Friendship is a gift, a special quality of relationship between people in which some of our social, emotional, and spiritual needs can be met. I think women have a special ability to build friendship and sisterhood, both individually and in Relief Society units.

Among the many reports we received of sesquicentennial service projects, a very touching one was from Cleo L. Evans, president of Spencer Fifth Ward in Magna. If you saw the broadcast of the Relief Society general meeting in 1993, you saw some video clips of Sister Evans explaining that the Relief Society sisters had decided to adopt a family who had special needs and made choosing such a family a matter of prayer. Several times they almost selected a family but each time felt that they should continue to look. They found that family when the bishop asked Sister Evans and one of her counselors to visit a nonmember family living in the ward boundaries whose twenty-three-month-old boy had died that morning of spinal meningitis. They discovered that the family

6

was in desperate financial need, the mother was pregnant, it was the father's birthday, and their car had broken down on the way home from the hospital after the toddler's death. They were bitter about God and also felt that Utah had "not been good" to them. Sister Evans and her counselor, without even speaking to each other, felt very strongly that this was their family.

Well, this is the kind of story that the Relief Society is famous for—but what impressed me the most was the list that the Relief Society president made of what the family needed. At the very top of that list was "friendship." Sister Evans recognized that the mother had been very lonely since the family had moved from California several months earlier. The women made a real commitment to meet that social and emotional need. That's a sensitivity that impresses me. Sometimes we do not recognize that there are unmet spiritual and emotional needs, even as we work gallantly to meet physical needs. Sometimes we leave souls hungry even while we feed bodies.

Friendship is built in little ways, with little acts of thoughtfulness and service. I think of one of our missionaries, Craig Moffat, now a doctor, who was our financial secretary. Ed assigned him to work with a companion who had been brought into the mission home because he was very discouraged and wanted to go home. One day Ed noticed that Craig looked very tired. Ed was always watching the faces of people. "Elder Moffat, are you all right?" he asked. "You look tired and out of energy. Tell me if there's anything that's going on." Elder Moffat reluctantly explained that he was fasting with and for his companion. In fact, they'd been fasting for the past three days.

Ed was both horrified and touched. He instantly said: "That's too long. You get right down to the kitchen and start eating. I'll talk to your companion." Yet, despite his concern, he was proud that Elder Moffat had had so much love and desire to serve in his heart that he would make this sacrifice for his companion.

Don't underestimate the power of your prayers in the lives of your friends. Kindness, love, and service are the foundations of friendship, but the crown of friendship is the special happiness that you have in each other's presence. And although I think that you can be friendly and cordial with almost everyone, there is a special holiness about true friendship. The trust in that relationship must not be violated or the friendship will be betrayed.

One woman who has the gift of friendship, in my opinion, is Fay Gaykowski, my neighbor and morning walking partner. Her husband, Richard, was our bishop for four years. They would have held a special place in our lives anyway, but getting to know them both and see them in action was a great privilege. All the years that Richard was bishop, Fay was an exceptional partner—observant, concerned, and supportive. I never heard her claim any special privileges as the bishop's wife, but rather she claimed special responsibilities to mother the ward. I know that she quietly paid attention to such things as bridal and baby showers. If it seemed that such a party was not materializing on its own, she found a friend to cohost it with her, and the ward had another opportunity for celebration.

As a neighbor and a friend, she has tended my plants and taken in the mail during the many assignments I have had that have required travel in the months since Ed's death. Frequently she and Richard have driven me to the airport or picked me up. My sense of homecoming has often started when I stepped on the escalator, looked down, and saw Fay standing at the foot, arms folded, waiting for me, with Richard outside at the curb. During our early morning walks, we share many things—burdens, problems, questions, and stresses—but somehow, with Fay, we also end up sharing strengths. And I know that Fay does the same thing for many women in our ward and in our community.

When Richard died of a cardiac arrest, this shared sorrow brought us even closer. I returned to Fay's side again and again during the time he was dying, during the funeral, and in the days and months that followed. I have earned the right to be at her side. Friendship gives me that cherished, honored place. I was so grateful to hear her say: "I'm really doing all right. I had a chance to observe you very closely in the months after Ed's death. I saw how you managed, how you kept yourself busy, and where you drew your strength from. I felt really prepared." I felt so grateful that I could give something to Fay, who had given so much to me.

Think for a moment about your friends. What are the bonds that make that relationship a strong, sweet one? What is precious and holy about it? How can you strengthen it, build it, cherish and honor it? A friendship can be a real sanctuary from an often stormy and demanding world.

But even very close friends do not always understand us. Even long-standing friendships can be interrupted by death or by people's moving away. Our truest sanctuary is a heart steadfastly fixed upon the Savior. That is a place of safety that requires no walls or doors. Family members may disappoint us. Time and distance may weaken the ties of the closest friendship. But nothing can change our Savior's love for us.

President James E. Faust once wrote an article on the kingdom of God that enhances my understanding of sanctuary:

> Thanks to my wonderful wife, the Spirit of the Lord has often been in our various dwelling-places. While we have lived within them, each has been a holy place for me. In our married life we have lived in single rooms with bathrooms down the hall and in small apartments. We have also owned three houses. In a sense, the Church has been in each, but I would not want to go back and live in our former houses, even though we spent much of our happy lives in them. The kingdom of God is not there. . . .
>
> Priesthood is desirable because whomsoever is blessed by this power, God will bless. But there have been many successful caring heads of families who are mothers, grandmothers, and others. What seems to distinguish a successful family is that the members of the family continue to care. They don't give up. They never quit. They hang together through hardships and death and other problems. . . .

The family is and must always be an important part of the Church. But the Lord's kingdom ultimately must be found in our hearts before it can be anywhere else.[4]

Our relationship with our Heavenly Father and with the Savior is a relationship that lies totally within our power to recognize, enhance, and enjoy in its full sweetness. That's because the Savior has already done more than half the work and is just waiting for us to come to him. We don't need to attract his attention or interest him in us. He already has us fully in his eye. He has been regarding us from eternity to eternity. We knew him in our premortal existence, and we chose the Father's plan because of our boundless trust in the Savior's promised atonement. He has fulfilled his pledge and stands ready to give us blessings, love, and peace in our hearts.

The Savior has already given us all of his love. We don't need to earn it. But I think it takes our whole lives to make that boundless love real in our limited perspective, to really believe in unconditional love with our very conditional minds and hearts. I think that's what being a disciple means—making a lifelong commitment to Christ.

Let me share with you an example of how I think that works. I've already told you about Fay Gaykowski. Let me tell you a little bit more about her husband, Richard. When he became bishop, we saw him step into that calling with his counselors' and Fay's support and just weave the ward together in love.

Bishop Gaykowski was a good listener who made people feel comfortable talking to him. He invited confidences with his trustworthiness, his willingness to help, and his steady, common-sense compassion. Looking for ways to help was an instinct with both him and Fay.

I cannot count the number of times that Ed said, "The bishop is a good man"—simple words, but a heartfelt accolade from one true disciple of Christ recognizing another. Ed always listened attentively to whatever Richard said as bishop. He took Richard's suggestions as applying to him personally and made serious efforts to implement them. When the bishop suggested that we set temple goals as individuals, Ed initiated his own schedule for going to the temple in addition to the evenings when we went as a couple. I'm convinced that Ed's last months were blessed by those extra hours of peace and spiritual preparation passed within the walls of the temple.

One of the most precious memories I have of Bishop Gaykowski is an experience he told me that communicates not only his style of leadership but also his testimony of the Savior. One Sunday had been especially challenging. From 6 A.M. to 6 P.M., with the only breaks being for more formal meetings, he had been meeting with people in trouble. A steady stream of ward members with problems, difficulties, perplexities, confusions, sins, and sorrows had come to his office and poured their troubles out before him. At the day's end, physically weary and burdened in soul with the troubles of his ward members, Bishop Gaykowski leaned his arms on his desk and dropped his head upon them, groaning within himself, "Why are all of these people coming to see me? What can I do?" This was the question in his mind when he raised his head and his eyes fell upon the portrait of the Savior that hung in his office. Clearly into his mind came the words, "They came to see me—through you."

Bishop Gaykowski was a disciple of Christ who knew that the ultimate sanctuary is our steadfast relationship with Christ.

We live in times of turmoil and menace. Our need for a sanctuary has never been greater. Homes, wards, and friendships can be places of sanctuary, but only if we develop in our hearts a sanctuary where God may dwell. In the sanctuary of our hearts, when our relationship with our Father in Heaven and with the Savior is steadfast and loving, then we can make other sanctuaries. We have the power and the motivation to make the covenants, nurture the relationships, and cherish the sanctity of our homes, our families, and our friendships—in our wards and beyond.

I feel to rejoice with the Psalmist in this fervent prayer of exultation and praise:

> O God, thou art my God; early will I seek thee: my soul thirsteth for thee, my flesh longeth for thee in a dry and thirsty land, where no water is;
>
> To see thy power and thy glory, so as I have seen thee in the sanctuary.
>
> Because thy lovingkindness is better than life, . . . my mouth shall praise thee with joyful lips:
>
> When I remember thee upon my bed, and meditate on thee in the night watches.
>
> Because thou hast been my help, therefore in the shadow of thy wings will I rejoice. (Psalm 63:1–7)

May we too rejoice!

2

TRUST IN THE LORD

Did you know that there are more than thirty references in the scriptures to trusting in the Lord? I think we're all familiar with the lovely scripture in Proverbs:

> Trust in the Lord with all thine heart; and lean not unto thine own understanding.
> In all thy ways acknowledge him, and he shall direct thy paths. (Proverbs 3:5–6)

But I found several others while I was exploring this topic. Consider these:

> Commune with your own heart. . . .
> Offer the sacrifices of righteousness, and put your trust in the Lord. (Psalm 4:4–5)
> It is better to trust in the Lord than to put confidence in man.
> It is better to trust in the Lord than to put confidence in princes. (Psalm 118:8–9)

And listen to these beautiful and powerful promises that are associated with trusting the Lord:

The Lord also will be a refuge for the oppressed, a refuge in times of trouble.

And they that know thy name will put their trust in thee: for thou, Lord, hast not forsaken them that seek thee. (Psalm 9:9–10)

Thou wilt keep him in perfect peace, whose mind is stayed on thee: because he trusteth in thee.

Trust ye in the Lord for ever: for in the Lord Jehovah is everlasting strength. (Isaiah 26:3–4)

Let me give you an analogy to show trust in the Lord. Think of a facial tissue and a handkerchief. As long as they're just waving in the breeze, both of them look alike. Both of them seem equally strong. You can blow your nose on both of them. You can even toss both of them in the washer, although you may not like what comes out! But let's say that you're in a situation in which you have to test that strength. Let's make it really dramatic. Suppose that my two-year-old grandson has slipped over the edge of a cliff and is caught on a narrow ledge several feet down—too far for me to reach or jump. I've tied together everything I could find in the car to make a rope long enough to reach him—the dog leash, an electrical extension cord, my panty hose, and it's still six inches too short. No matter how I strain, and no matter how high Andrew stretches, we just can't make contact. Then I find this tissue and this handkerchief. Which one am I going to use to make the rope longer? That's not a very tough question, is it? I know from experience that no ordinary effort can rip the handkerchief, but it doesn't even take trying hard to turn the tissue into shreds.

The point I'm trying to make is that we need to have a trust in the Lord that we can count on, one that springs from deep faith and has been tested by our own experience. There are going to be trials and adversities in our lives. We can't be rich enough or smart enough or healthy enough to avoid trials. All we can be is strong enough to withstand them when they come, and that strength comes from the Savior.

We can trust our Savior in a way that we can trust no other living being. Even the best of human relationships is limited. Can we trust our mothers to be there when troubles come? Not always. Even if they were willing, they are sometimes unable to help because of distance, poverty, other obligations, or illness. Can we trust the Lord to be there when troubles come? Yes, we can.

Can we trust our friends to listen to us when we're upset about something? Not always. Our friends may be out of town. Their line may be busy. Or even if they're sympathetic, they may see the issue in a very different way. Can we trust the Lord to listen to us when we need to talk to him? Yes, we can.

Can we trust our spouses to sense when we're lonely or sad, and to know what to do about it? Not always. Our spouses may be overwhelmed by their own responsibilities. Can we trust the Lord to understand our needs and to be with us? Yes, we can. He will not always solve our problems for us, but he will be with us while we deal with them. He will give us the courage, the love, and the peace that we need to keep on going, even if the burden is not one that can be lifted.

We can't rely on someone else's faith in the Savior. We can't depend on someone else to get answers to prayers for us. We can't ask someone else to listen to the whisperings of the Holy Ghost for us. We have to do it ourselves. Nor can we do it for anyone else. We can pray that our children will develop faith in the Savior, and we can testify of our own faith, but we cannot give them our faith. We can pray for inspiration for our friends, but we very seldom are authorized to receive answers for them. Occasionally we may receive the insight that a person needs to understand a puzzling situation, but we cannot listen to the Holy Ghost for that person. We each have to carry our own oil for our own lamps.

Let me tell you a story about trust. Once I went to Wisconsin to tend my two little grandsons while my son and daughter-in-law hunted hard for a house in Denver. Six-year-old Matthew and I were good buddies, but it was my first opportunity to spend a long period of time with two-year-old Andrew. Bob, my son, had already gone to Denver to begin work, leaving his wife, Chris, behind to sell the house. It's hard to be without your daddy when you're only two, even if he does telephone every evening. How are you going to feel when Mom disappears too?

So I had special concerns about Andrew. He cried when Chris left, but I cuddled him and, in a few minutes, got out a storybook that proved to be a good distraction. And we settled down to our routine for the next four days—if you can say that you *have* a routine when you're living with a two-year-old! My goodness! I decided Heavenly Father was very smart to send two-year-olds to *young* women!

The next morning when Andrew woke up, he called out. Did he call for his daddy? No, he didn't. Did he call for his mom? No, he called, "Nana!" Somehow in his mind he knew, even waking up from a night's sleep, that he was safe with someone who loved him and would take care of him. He somehow knew that he could trust me. The next morning, he again called, "Nana!" When his mother telephoned, you could tell that he loved her and missed her. Big tears rolled down his cheeks as he listened to her voice on the telephone, but he was easy to comfort afterwards and again, on Sunday morning, he called, "Nana!" Then, on Sunday night, Chris came home. Monday morning, when Andrew woke up, he called, "Mama!" He knew that his mother had come home, and his trust could repose safely in her.

It made me think of that scripture, "My sheep hear my voice, and I know them, and they follow me" (John 10:27). The trust of a two-year-old is precious. Andrew knew whether it was his mother or his grandmother who was caring for him. I felt honored that he could trust me to be there for him on the mornings when his mother could not be. In the same way, when we have a personal and individual relationship with the Lord, we have learned to recognize his voice and listen to it when it comes. We can trust him to always answer us—no matter what our circumstances.

This earth is not a vacation resort for the redeemed but a hospital for the ailing. Mortality was planned as an experience in dealing with failures as well as triumphs. We feel pain when our bodies fail to work properly. We become tired and make hasty judgments or speak impatiently to others. We feel burdened with the demands, the unfriendliness, the sorrows of family members and neighbors. Financial trials arise, and we face the reality of bills piling up. Knowledge of all these physical realities comes to us through our senses.

A strong faith in the Savior does not require us to deny these realities or to say they're not important. Instead, faith asks us to go forward in spite of these realities. Think of Peter who, with his friends, had spent the entire night fishing. Then Jesus told him to let down the net on the other side of the boat. Peter was a professional. He and his friends had grown up on the Sea of Galilee. He knew about currents, the feeding habits of fish, and the best times to catch fish. He also knew that the water on one side of the boat was a lot like the water on the other side of the boat. He explained to Jesus, respectfully but candidly, that they had been fishing all night without luck. Then he added, "Nevertheless at thy word I will let down the net." So he did, and he caught so many fish that the net broke (Luke 5:5–6).

Now, it's interesting to me that Jesus didn't scold Peter for his lack of faith. He listened patiently to Peter's description of the facts. They were, after all, facts. But Peter did his part, too. When he was sure that Jesus, a carpenter, hadn't accidentally overlooked any of the facts important to a fisherman, he let down his net and gathered in his reward. I think Peter could do this because he had already had enough spiritual experience with Jesus to know that there was something beyond material reality to consider.

Remember that the goal of faith is not a problem-free life. The goal of faith is salvation. When we have a problem, we may give God a list of what his possible action plans might be, but he is not limited to our thinking.

The testimonies of our latter-day prophets are also strengthening. I read with great comfort the counsel of President Ezra Taft Benson, given specifically and especially to single sisters. Over and over again, he sends us to the source of real strength. Listen to these affirmations:

> Trust in the Lord. [There is that counsel again!] Be assured He loves you and we love you. . . .
>
> Establish a deep and abiding relationship with the Lord Jesus Christ. Know that He is there—always there. Reach out to Him. He does answer prayers. He does bring peace. He does give hope. In the words of the Psalmist: "He is my refuge and my fortress: . . . in him will I trust" (Psalm 91:2). Study carefully the life of the Savior. He is our great exemplar. . . .
>
> Your individual worth as a daughter of God transcends all. . . .
>
> If . . . you . . . are worthy and endure faithfully, you can be assured of all blessings from a kind and loving Heavenly Father—and I emphasize *all blessings.*
>
> God has your eternal perspective in mind. . . .
>
> Realize the strength of your inner self and that, with God's help, you "can do all things through Christ which strengtheneth [you]" (Philippians 4:1). . . .
>
> Dwell upon the goodness of the Lord to you. . . .
>
> My humble desire . . . is that you will receive all that the Father hath, "even an hundred fold, yea, more." And I promise you that indeed you will.[1]

We can trust the Savior, but do we? I want to talk about honesty because I think it's a simple fact that we can trust in the Lord with all our hearts only if we have clean hands and a pure heart. And one of the most important ways we can be pure before the Lord is to be scrupulously honest in our words and deeds.

The first person we need to be honest with is with the Lord. The Lord doesn't want just pretty prayers. He wants real prayers. Sometimes we think of those eloquent, gracious prayers in sacrament meeting and general conference as the models for our personal prayers. We try to organize our rough thoughts into smooth sentences and it seems hard. We know how to say, "I'm so grateful for our son who is on his mission," but we might not know how to say, "I'm so scared and so mad about our son who is on drugs." Heavenly Father wants to hear the scared and mad prayers just as much as he wants to hear the grateful prayers.

Sometimes it's very hard for us to be honest, especially with negative feelings and ideas. Elder Neal A. Maxwell asked a soul-searching question: "Can we partake of tiny, bitter cups without becoming bitter?"[2] I think we can, with God's help, but not if we deny that the cup is bitter in the first place.

When Jesus was praying in the Garden of Gethsemane, he was honest about how hard the Atonement was going to be for him when he prayed that the cup might pass from him. He struggled with a "very heavy" burden of feelings, saying, "My soul is exceeding sorrowful unto death," and he prayed, "Father, all things are possible unto thee; take away this cup from me" (Mark 14:33–34, 36). He was honest about how much he *didn't* like what was happening; and I think it's because of his honesty that we so revere the love and humility revealed by the rest of his prayer: "Nevertheless not what I will, but what thou wilt" (Mark 14:36).

Can we be equally honest in our prayers? Remember, we're not going to shock our Father in Heaven. There isn't anything we can say that he hasn't already heard, nothing we can show him that he hasn't already seen. We may shock ourselves a little when we start being honest, but I think some very profound revelations come to us in those moments.

I read a personal essay by one woman who felt terrified and shattered when her marriage of almost twenty-five years ended in divorce. But one of the important things that helped her live through it was being completely honest about what it meant to her. She explains:

> Divorce entails a whole series of losses. Besides the obvious loss of a spouse, divorced people often lose their identity, their place in the family/church/community, their economic status

and financial security, their faith in other people and God, and their belief that the future will be happier. Telling yourself to ignore the pain . . . is counterproductive.

Probably the single most important step toward healing I took, was learning to look honestly at the situation and to grieve well. Only by doing so could I become mentally strong and emotionally whole.

. . . I listed the ways I had been affected. Eventually, with the help of a close friend, my minister, and my support group, I admitted my anger and pain over each loss.

This is hard to do because people praise us when we seem able to put hard experiences behind us and go on. Maybe you have had people ask, "How are you?" obviously hoping that the answer will be, "Fine," because they're not quite sure what they'd say if you said, "I feel terrible," or started to cry. This same writer had this advice for others who are caught in traumatic situations:

> Don't be ashamed to weep over what you have lost; feeling is essential to forgiving. One thing that helped me, once I had learned to release my emotions and cry again, was to limit myself to, say, five or ten minutes of weeping, especially when grief overwhelmed me during the working day. For a few moments I would shut the office door; after my allotted time, I would wash my face and resume work. Crying purged away a great deal of the pain.[3]

I think her suggestion is a wonderful combination of honesty and trust. It honestly acknowledges when things hurt and lets you grieve over them, and it expresses the trust that you're stronger than the pain. You won't fall apart if you let yourself weep. You *can* pull yourself together and get on with your responsibilities and duties.

People talk about grief being paralyzing, but I don't think anything is as paralyzing as denial—as lying to ourselves about what hurts. How can healing start without an acknowledgment of what has happened to us? How can we ever move to the point of forgiveness if we try to explain a trial away as a mistake or a misunderstanding or our own fault for being oversensitive? We need to be honest with ourselves and we need to be honest with our feelings.

Honesty isn't a license to go out and beat up on people emotionally. Why is it that when people say, "I'm going to be perfectly honest with you," we know that they're going to say something unpleasant? Well, it's sometimes hard to be honest and it's sometimes hard to hear honest statements. It seems harsh and unloving to say things people don't want to hear.

But I think one key is to talk only about what's in our own hearts. We don't get to talk about what's in someone else's heart, what someone else is thinking, what someone else's motives might be.

The scriptures tell us how to balance the demands of truth and love. When the apostle Paul was explaining to the Ephesian Saints about how members of congregations were supposed to relate to each other and help each other grow, he said:

> Speaking the truth in love, may [you] grow up into him in all things, which is the head, even Christ:
>
> From whom the whole body fitly joined together and compacted by that which every joint supplieth, according to the effectual working in the measure of every part, maketh increase of the body unto the edifying of itself in love. (Ephesians 4:15–16)

It's the part about "speaking the truth in love" that I want us to focus on. What is he saying? If Paul were writing today, perhaps he might use language like this:

> By speaking the truth in a spirit of love, we must grow up in every way to Christ, who is the head.

21

Under his control all the different parts of the body fit together, and the whole body is held together by every joint with which it is provided. So when each separate part works as it should, the whole body grows and builds itself up through love.

Think for a minute about Joseph who was sold into Egypt. The first words we hear him speak, as recorded in the scriptures, are a recitation to his brothers about his dream of the eleven sheaves bowing down to his sheaf, which his brothers immediately (and correctly!) interpreted as meaning that he would rule over them. And then he dreamed a second dream in which the sun, the moon, and eleven stars bowed down to him. At this, even his father was upset, asking, "Shall I and thy mother and thy brethren indeed come to bow down ourselves to thee to the earth?" (Genesis 37:7–10).

Now, was Joseph telling the truth? Certainly. So the problem wasn't his honesty at all. But was he telling the truth *in love?* Was he telling this truth to help his family get along better and to establish a better relationship with his brothers? He was very young; I wonder if maybe he naively thought that if his brothers knew he was going to be so important, they'd stop envying him because his father loved him the best (which in itself was quite a problem). Or is it possible that Joseph was speaking the truth in pride?

Sometimes we tell our children the exact truth about themselves: "You haven't made your bed for three days, you've been totally grouchy at every single meal since Sunday, you haven't been on time for seminary once this week, and I'm just so relieved when you're at school." Now, every single one of those statements may be totally honest, but does it pass the love test? This sounds to me like a mother who is speaking the truth in exasperation, not in love. We can feel the difference when someone says, "You know, my dear, I have to tell you how it makes me feel when I saw your bed unmade this morning for the third day in a row and listened to you complain about the toast and call your brother names during breakfast, just as you did yesterday and the day before." Same facts—different feelings.

Speaking to the students at Brigham Young University, Elder L. Tom Perry stressed the concept of honesty in an impressive way:

> You might ask, how can we be completely honest? To be completely honest, we must look carefully at our lives and have the courage to face the whole truth. If there are ways in which we are being even the least bit dishonest, we should begin at once to repent from them. When we are completely honest, we cannot be corrupted. We are true to every trust, duty, agreement, and covenant, even if it costs us money, friends, or our lives. Then we can face the Lord, ourselves, and others without shame.[4]

We've talked about how the Lord is the only being whom we can ultimately trust, because he is the only person who has the power to keep every promise that he makes and the only one who has the ability to act always out of love instead of more conflicted motives. But our goal in mortality is to emulate Christ, and that means becoming as trustworthy as he is. I love the description of the virtuous woman in Proverbs 31:11, "The heart of her husband doth safely trust in her." Isn't that a wonderful thing to be able to say about another person? Can the heart of your friend safely trust in you? Can the heart of your children safely trust in you? Can the heart of your visiting teaching companion safely trust in you?

Let me give you just one example, reported by an anonymous person about his father, of how individual honesty can impact society. He wrote:

> A man entered my father's diesel-repair shop, said he was a driver from a trucking fleet and suggested, "How about adding a few extra parts to the bill? We'll let the company pay for it, and you and I can split the difference."

Dad refused, but the customer was insistent. "I come through here a lot," the man continued. "We could make quite a bit of money." Dad said that wasn't how he operated.

"Everyone does it!" the man yelled. "Are you some kind of fool?" Burning mad, Dad asked him to leave and take his business elsewhere.

Suddenly the man smiled and extended his hand for a handshake. "I own a trucking company," he said. "I've been looking for a mechanic I can trust, and I'm not taking my business anywhere else!"[5]

Isn't that a wonderful example? Of course, things don't always work out so well. Elder Perry tells us honestly that honesty may cost us money, friends, and even our lives. But as Saints of God, we simply don't have the option of telling the truth only when it's convenient or comfortable. Honesty can't be selective. All that we have to give back to God at the end of our lives is our characters. If we have spent our lives living a lie or being one person on the outside but another person on the inside, then we have taken the Savior's gift of complete atonement and perfect love and have given him a flawed gift in return, not a whole heart that can be healed and sanctified.

A dual responsibility accompanies honesty. The first is the responsibility of courage. The second is the responsibility of charity. We must have the courage to speak the truth of our own experience, our own hearts, our own minds, and our own spirits. And then we must have the charity to listen to others share the truths of their own experience.

I think this process will take patience. We need to be patient as we find loving ways to say things that may sound hard to other people. We need to be patient as we listen to things that we may not agree with from others. We need to remember that we don't need to judge, we don't need to fix, we don't need to agree, and we definitely don't need to give advice. We just need to listen and try to understand.

A church in downtown Salt Lake City displayed this inspirational thought on its notice board: "The most important things in life are not things." We believe that, don't we? We believe that the most important thing we can give to God, to the Church, and to our families is who we really are. Limited, yes. Flawed and with a long list of failings, yes. But an eternal and noble spirit from the premortal existence who chose to walk the path of faith and who voted for the risks of the Savior's plan of freedom and love, not Satan's plan of total obedience and non-growth.

We have nothing to fear from the truth. The truth may demand sacrifices of us and hold us to high standards, but that is a price we should be willing to pay. Truth has the power to transform lives. That's why honesty is so utterly important. Let me tell you one final story. When I was a school principal, one of my sixth-graders—I'll call him David—came to class with a spectacular black eye. He said he had run into something, but it was obviously from a blow. And because of the family situation, I felt we needed to report it as a case of child abuse.

I knew his mother fairly well, because we'd had several encounters during that school year. The first meeting we'd had was when David was attending another school and I felt he would do better in our school, which was his neighborhood school. I can't remember what I said, but it touched her heart and changed her mind, so she agreed to have him transferred to our school. I kept in touch with her as the months passed, and so did the teacher. She was initially very withdrawn, but with each meeting she talked more freely, until at this point we had a fairly open relationship.

So that afternoon, I saw her peek around the corner of my door. I called, "Come in and sit down! I know why you're here."

"Yes," she said. "I got a call from the social worker."

I looked her in the eye. "I want you to know that your son tried to protect you."

"Well," she said defiantly, "I boxed him in the face."

I wasn't shocked. I didn't scold or lecture her. I just said, "I thought that was what had happened, but he tried to tell us that he'd had an accident."

She looked confused and a little helpless. I knew that she hadn't meant to hurt him, and that her own anger and violence were as frightening to her as they were to David.

I continued, "Some of the things that happen are difficult to talk about. But it's wrong for people to hit kids, and you know it."

She nodded.

"So tell me what I can do to help you help your son."

We talked about David. We talked about her. We talked about her work with her therapist. David was a wonderful boy—handsome, intelligent, and a hard worker. And his mother continued to make progress as the months passed.

When I was going to leave that school, she came and hugged me in tears, then wrote me the nicest letter saying that I was the first person who had ever trusted her. She felt trusted because I had been honest with her. Would that have happened if we'd accepted the boy's story and pretended nothing was wrong? Would she have trusted me if I hadn't told her what was in my heart? I don't think so.

Out of the many beautiful scriptures that the tenderhearted apostle John wrote, I think one that shows his personal love is in his epistle to a nameless woman and her children. Notice how closely truth and love are interwoven in this salutation:

> The elder unto the elect lady and her children, whom I love in the truth; and not I only, but also all they that have known the truth;
>
> For the truth's sake, which dwelleth in us, and shall be with us for ever.
>
> Grace be with you, mercy, and peace, from God the Father, and from the Lord Jesus Christ, the Son of the Father, in truth and love. (2 John 1:1–3)

I pray the same blessings upon us all as we trust in the Lord, approach him with pure hearts, speak the truth in love, and devote our efforts to creating islands of honesty from which we can build bridges of honest communication to others. May our hearts trust in him, and may we have his perfect peace as we live in truth and in love.

3

DOORS AND THRESHOLDS

I was up very early one morning working, and when I looked out of my window toward the east where the light was beginning to glow behind the mountains, the phrase came to my mind, "the gates of day." That got me thinking about doors and thresholds. Now, we do things with all kinds of doors every day without thinking—revolving doors, glass doors, wooden doors, doors with crash bars, doors we lock behind us with keys, doors in restroom stalls that have latches to keep them shut for privacy, car doors, doors sealed with yellow tape in police investigations.

I think of the majestic and beautifully carved great doors on the east side of the Salt Lake Temple. These doors are probably the most photographed doors in Salt Lake City, because so many young couples getting married or older couples being sealed commemorate that event with photographs in front of them—but these doors are never photographed open because they guard the sacred interior of the House of the Lord. Think of the wooden doors that lead into the interior of the Assembly Hall and the Tabernacle. They're modernized, yet an effort is made to keep them harmonious with the pioneer style of the buildings which they serve. Think of the gates that lead into Temple Square— strong, capable of being locked for security, open so that what goes on beyond them can be seen and so that they convey an invitation both to come in and to go out.

We probably don't pay much attention to doors, do we? The reason doors seldom get much scrutiny is because their thresholds are not stopping places. They're transition points. We seldom really notice doors because we're always on our way through them or past them or waiting for them to open. Doors are not destinations. They're markers on the way to our destinations. Thresholds are places of waiting, of expectancy, even of crisis. Doors are open to permit free passage, or closed to bar the way. And all of them have hinges.

I've read the scriptures with a great deal of enjoyment, thinking of the images of doors and thresholds that they present. I'm sure we all immediately think of that tender and evocative statement of the Savior's: "Behold, I stand at the door, and knock: if any man [or woman] hear my voice, and open the door, I will come in . . . and will sup with him [or her], and he [or she] with me" (Revelation 3:20). You've seen the famous painting that shows Christ standing patiently at the door, his hand still lifted from knocking, his head tilted, listening for the sound of the footsteps of someone coming to open the door for him. You've likely noticed the significance of the artist's choice to paint the door without a handle or a latch or a doorknob on the exterior so that the only way the door can be opened is from the interior. Allowing Christ to enter our lives, the artist is saying, must be our choice, because he cannot force himself upon us.

There are two additional passages of scripture I'd like to call to your attention about similar situations: of someone standing outside the door and knocking. Jesus warned his apostles about the need for prompt repentance and timely righteousness, because the days were limited in which such action could be taken.

When once the master of the house is risen up, and hath shut to the door, and ye begin to stand without, and to knock at the door, saying, Lord, Lord, open unto us; and he shall answer and say unto you, I know you not whence ye are:

Then shall ye begin to say, We have eaten and drunk in thy presence, and thou hast taught in our streets.

But he shall say, I tell you, I know you not whence ye are; depart from me, all ye workers of iniquity.

There shall be weeping and gnashing of teeth, when ye shall see Abraham, and Isaac, and Jacob, and all the prophets, in the kingdom of God, and you yourselves thrust out.

And they shall come from the east, and from the west, and from the north, and from the south, and shall sit down in the kingdom of God.

And, behold, there are last which shall be first, and there are first which shall be last. (Luke 13:25–30)

This passage is a powerful one to me for two reasons. First, it reminds me that there is no work more important for me than to do the works of righteousness every day, to repent of my sins, to ask for forgiveness, to pray, and to serve others so that I may be a true disciple of the Savior and so that he will recognize me. But the second message is that it is not for me to judge the righteousness of others. The Lord is the master of the house. He knows who has served him wholeheartedly, while others who claim his acquaintance in the street or even to have been intimate friends who have eaten at his table have hearts that are far from him and cannot be permitted to enter his presence at the last day. I am the only person who can make my heart right before the Lord.

And the second story of someone knocking at the door is a delightful one, the story of Peter's miraculous escape from prison as recounted in Acts 12. This story occurred during a time when Herod was actively persecuting the Christians. "He killed James the brother of John with the sword. And because he saw it pleased the Jews, he proceeded further to take Peter also." He imprisoned him under a heavy guard, "but prayer was made without ceasing of the church unto God for him." And this is a point I'd like to stress: faith opens doors. Because listen to what happened.

On the very night before Herod planned to have Peter executed, he was asleep "between two soldiers, bound with two chains" and other soldiers guarded the prison doors. You wonder what kind of sleep Peter could have under those circumstances, and perhaps he wasn't sleeping very well, uncomfortable in his chains, with two men close beside him.

And an angel appeared in the prison, surrounded by a light, and awakened Peter by hitting him in the side. Needless to say, Peter woke up, and when he stood up, the chains fell away from him.

Then, while Peter stood there, probably blinking in the light, the angel said something like: "Get dressed. Where are your shoes? What have you done with your cloak?" I just have to laugh when I read this because the angel sounds like a frazzled parent trying to get children ready for school and out the door in time to catch the school bus.

And when Peter was finally ready, the angel gave him another order: "Follow me." By this time, Peter had figured it out. He decided he was having a dream. The scripture says, "And [he] wist not that it was true which was done by the angel; but thought he saw a vision."

So they passed the first set of guards, then the second set. By this time, Peter must have been thinking, "This is a great dream! I don't mind this at all!" Then "they came unto the iron gate that leadeth unto the city; which opened to them of his own accord." But then suddenly, after they'd passed the first street, the angel disappeared, and Peter realized that he really was awake—that it wasn't a dream.

His heart was filled with gratitude and awe at this miracle, and he said, "Now I know of a surety, that the Lord hath sent his angel, and hath delivered me out of the hand of Herod, and from all the expectation of the people of the Jews."

But there he was, standing in the street. The angel had gotten

31

him out of prison, but now he had to make a few decisions. Certainly, one option was to stand there in the street marveling at his miraculous escape until the soldiers woke up, noticed he was gone, and came looking for him. It probably didn't take much thought to reject that option. What he did was come straight to the Saints, who were meeting in the house of Mary the mother of John surnamed Mark, "where many were gathered together praying."

And here's where the second amusing episode of this event takes place. Peter stood on the threshold and knocked on the locked "door of the gate," which I envision as a person-sized door set in the larger gates that could open to let through wagons or other large vehicles.

The person who answered the door was a young woman named Rhoda. Rhoda was so overcome with amazement and joy when she recognized Peter's voice outside the gate that she immediately lost her head. Instead of letting him in, she ran back into the meeting and told everyone that Peter was at the gate.

Naturally, there was a certain amount of skepticism. In fact, the other people in the meeting said, "Thou art mad." But she insisted that it really was Peter. Then someone suggested that it must be his "angel," which I think means his spirit. Meanwhile, Peter was still standing at the door, patiently knocking—or maybe impatiently. I think he could be forgiven if he were perhaps getting a little upset. Finally someone had a third idea: open the door and see if he really was there. So they did.

And guess what? According to the scriptures, "They were astonished," and they must have all begun talking at once, because Peter signaled to them "to hold their peace." Then he delivered *his* message: He told them how the Lord had brought him out of the prison, ordered them to report these things to "James, and to the brethren," and then, very prudently, "he departed, and went into another place."

And just for the sake of keeping a conscientious record, the scriptures add this P.S. that makes me smile: "Now as soon as it was day, there was no small stir among the soldiers, what was become of Peter" (Acts 12:1–18).

Now, this is a story of doors and thresholds. Peter had to cross the threshold of sleep into wakefulness, even though he thought he still slept. Passively, he obeyed the angel's instructions and followed him, as if in a dream, across the threshold of the prison cell, out of the prison itself, and through the gates that led into the street. Once in the street, the angel disappeared and Peter had to cross another threshold of perception, acknowledging to himself that he was awake. He could no longer be passive at that point. He had to take action.

This action—the decision to go to Mary's house—brought him to another threshold. This time, there was no angel to convey him effortlessly across that threshold and into the circle of friends who were praying for his deliverance. He had to make his own way there, and it seems to have been astonishingly hard work. First, he had to make somebody hear him. Then he had to put up with Rhoda who, amazed by the miracle and confused by love, did exactly the wrong thing and left him standing on the threshold while she bore the good news into the inner room that their prayers had been answered.

Then what happened? Instead of welcoming this much-desired message, these Saints scolded the messenger and accused her of being crazy. When she persisted, someone came up with a tortuous explanation to account for the appearance of Peter—it was his angel. I just wonder how long this comedy went on until someone suggested the obvious: "Let's check it out." And when they did, Peter had to take strong measures to get them to pay attention to this manifestation of God's love more than to their own reactions and astonishment.

Don't you love what this story shows about human nature? Sometimes our most sincere prayers are answered by totally miraculous means, but there almost always comes a point where the angel leaves us and we must use our own agency, our own willpower, and our own decision-making abilities. Or think of the position of the Saints in Mary's house. It was the middle of the night and they had obviously been praying for hours that Peter would be spared. But when it happened, they didn't believe it. They denied that it had happened. They tried to explain it away. To actually accept the miracle by looking at it was the last thing they did, and then they were so overwhelmed with their own reactions that they couldn't even welcome Peter properly. Their prayer of faith brought the miracle to their doorstep, but for a long, suspenseful moment they lacked the final ounce of faith to open the door and let the miracle enter.

When we stand on the threshold of crisis, do we have enough faith to knock on the door? Mother Teresa tells about her first, frightening day on the streets of Calcutta after leaving the Sisters of Loreto, the convent where she had taught school. In later years, she saw that day as a test of her willingness to be faithful—to knock on a door when she was so poor that there wasn't even a threshold. She says:

> A priest came up to me. He asked me to give a contribution to a collection for the Catholic press. I had left with five rupees, and I had given four of them to the poor. I hesitated, then gave the priest the one that remained. That afternoon, the same priest came to see me and brought an envelope. He told me that a man had given him the envelope because he had heard about my projects and wanted to help me. There were fifty rupees in the envelope. I had the feeling, at that moment, that God had begun to bless the work and would never abandon me.[1]

We all know the great miracles wrought by the faith of Mother Teresa and those who work with her. She has heard the knock on her door and has opened it to the homeless, the needy, and the ill of India. Will our faith bring us to face the doors we need knock on, even if it means standing on a very uncomfortable threshold?

I think as Latter-day Saints we have a special feeling for the opening of doors because we have all seen such miracles, just within the last few years, as the promise of the Doctrine and Covenants is literally fulfilled in the opening of long-closed doors to missionary work. In Doctrine and Covenants 107:35 we read that "the Twelve [are] sent out, holding the keys, to open the door by the proclamation of the gospel of Jesus Christ, and first unto the Gentiles and then unto the Jews."

Elsewhere he gave a promise that has cheered the hearts of many weary missionaries: "Behold, and lo, I have much people in this place, in the regions round about; and an *effectual door* shall be opened in the regions round about in this eastern land." (I don't know about you, but I had to look up *effectual* in the dictionary. It means "producing the desired result"—which certainly makes it the right word in this context!) Then the Lord instructs us to declare the gospel "in my name, in solemnity of heart, in the spirit of meekness, in all things. And I give unto you this promise, that . . . the Holy Ghost shall be shed forth in bearing record unto all things whatsoever ye shall say" (D&C 100:3, 7–8; emphasis added).

We are all member-missionaries. We all represent the Church. We all are guardians of the light of the gospel—in our own lives, in the lives of our children, in the lives of our families and friends. Surely this is a promise that we want to claim—that in our contacts with loved ones, friends, and strangers we can open an effectual door and the Holy Ghost will be shed forth as we speak in meekness and conviction about our Savior.

Of course, we also increase our faith by praying, by making and keeping our baptismal and temple covenants, by holding family home evening, by serving others willingly, by accepting and magnifying our callings, and by feasting daily on the scriptures. If we are faithful in the performance of these duties, our faith *will* increase. And through the miracle of Christ's love and grace and mercy, these duties somehow lose any element of drudgery they might have had. Prayer becomes a never-ending, satisfying communication with a beloved and loving friend. The scriptures become sweet to us. Service becomes an instinct. Covenanting becomes a privilege. The Lord gives us commandments that will strengthen us, and then gives us the strength to keep those commandments.

Let me make one more point about doors. They turn on hinges. I don't know what the hinges are in your life, but to me, a major hinge is prayer. As the hymn reminds us, "Prayer can change the night to day." What changes night to day for you? For me, it's prayer. It brings about daily miracles.

Think of the line in the Lord's Prayer, "Give us this day our daily bread." Why does the prayer say the bread of "this day" and not the bread of "tomorrow"? Could it be because God wants us to come to him tomorrow likewise? If we already had tomorrow's bread, is it possible that we would fail to ask Heavenly Father for it? One writer points out, "Our greatest misery is really not want and pain, but distance from God. [Thus,] our extra loaf would really be a curse instead of a blessing; like the extra manna in the wilderness, it would only rot in our hands."[2] Daily prayer, even hourly prayer, is the bread that nourishes our souls.

Let me tell you a missionary story about prayer that came to me recently in a letter from Cherill and Jack Warnock. They're friends who were serving a mission in Fort Apache, Arizona. Cherill said a new elder had recently been assigned to their district.

> He was a farm boy from Idaho, and we don't think he was very anxious to come out. He's the first in his family to do so. The last three weeks have been difficult ones for him, wracked with homesickness and a certain degree of humiliation at being a greenie. Those things are surprisingly hard on a young fellow who was a big-time senior, who raced his car up and down the main street of some podunk town just a few months ago. He has suddenly discovered that he is not nearly as independent, important, or significant a person as he had himself figured to be just a very few short weeks ago.
>
> He told us that he was totally disgusted and thinking of throwing in the towel. Here he was walking the streets of a

strange town where a lot of the people have absolutely no interest in him and what he has to say. He was even wondering if the Lord had any interest in him. He was sort of argumentative in his prayers. "Just show me one person that this is benefiting," he told the Lord, "and I'll consider sticking around."

The Lord definitely heard him. The next couple of days he received a letter from his father up on the farm. The family had been in debt all of the boys' life; he knew that. They always made a living; but what with up and down crop years, they just couldn't seem to get money ahead. The father always had to borrow money to operate, and the debt seemed to hang permanently over their heads.

"You wouldn't believe what has happened since you left," the father wrote. "We've never gotten over sixty dollars a crate for our onions; this year they shot up over a hundred. Remember those new potatoes we planted to see what they would do: Well, they produced three times what the oldest ones did, and we get a much better price for them. Even the grain has made money this year. That's the first time it's done that in years! We're out of debt, son, we're out of debt," his father continued, "and we're putting money in the bank already with more to come. I can't believe it. I just can't believe it."

My friends said, "[The missionary] wept as he told us. . . . And I'm afraid we were a little dewy-eyed ourselves. The smart-alecky kid who raced his car up and down the street was starting to turn into a man in front of our eyes. 'I guess I know now who it's benefiting,' he said."[3]

Sometimes you may feel that you stand on the threshold of adversity and that the door before you is so thick and so heavy that no one on the other side is listening. Sometimes you may feel that your knuckles are bloody from knocking. Sometimes you feel lonely, left out, shut out. Please believe me when I tell you that you are not standing on that threshold alone. The Savior is standing beside you. His arm is around your shoulders, offering his support. His hand is uplifted to knock at the same time yours is. In his face is the same weariness and patience and endurance as yours. You are not alone. You are not forsaken even in your hardest moments.

Could I ask you to continue in faith if you feel that you are on the outside of the door? Lift your eyes in faith to the Savior, who is your companion on that threshold, and be comforted in that companionship. And if you are on the inside of the door, will you please listen carefully for knockings? Those knockings may be timid, coming from one who is not sure if she will be welcome. That knock may be faint, from someone who is so discouraged that she is just about to turn away. You may be very busy with your housekeeping. There may even be an important meeting going on, and the knock may seem like an interruption. Please remember that an angel may have brought this person to your door. Do not leave someone outside who yearns to be included.

We all deal with many individuals. Each one of those contacts is precious. If you only have one minute, make each of those sixty seconds count. Let me quote Mother Teresa one more time. She says:

> I do not agree with the big way of doing things. To us what matters is an individual. To get to love the person we must come in close contact with him. If we must wait till we get the numbers, then we will be lost in the numbers. And we will never be able to show that love and respect for the person. I believe in person to person; every person is Christ for me, and since there is only one Jesus, that person is the only person in the world for me at that moment. . . . What we are doing is just a drop in the ocean. But if that drop was not in the ocean I think the ocean will be less, because of that missing drop.[4]

I remember reading about a wonderful example of what happens when we pay attention to the little drops of water, to individuals. According to the report in the *Ensign* of the Tabernacle

Choir's 1993 tour of Israel, part of the incredible success they enjoyed in that country came about because of an individual act of kindness by an unknown usher at the Tabernacle many years earlier. This is what happened:

Iain B. McKay, director of international media relations for Bonneville Communications, recognized the importance of making the music of the choir available to everyone. Radio and television broadcasts are an important source of music for those living in Israel and the surrounding area. Therefore, Iain's meeting in Jerusalem with Avi Hanani, head of music for the Israel Broadcasting Authority (the umbrella organization for Israeli radio and television, and the Jerusalem Symphony), was a very important event.

"Robert Cundick, Tabernacle organist emeritus, attended the meeting with me," says Brother McKay. "We walked in, and I handed my card to Mr. Hanani. When he saw Salt Lake City on the card he said, 'Let me tell you about Salt Lake City.'"

Mr. Hanani proceeded to tell them about his own experience at Temple Square thirty-two years earlier. During the summer, his family toured the western United States and stopped at Salt Lake City. A music student, sixteen-year-old Avi got up early the next morning to visit the Tabernacle and hear the Tabernacle Choir's broadcast of "Music and the Spoken Word." When he got there, all the doors were locked, but he could see through a window that the choir was rehearsing. Timidly, he began knocking on each door, and at about the fifth door an usher opened it. Avi simply said, "I am a music student from Jerusalem and I'd like to hear the choir." At that point, the usher could have told the young man to come back later. Instead, he invited him in. The rehearsal stopped, and Richard P. Condie, the conductor of the choir, shook hands with Avi, introduced him to the choir, and invited him to sit in one of the empty choir seats and listen. When the rehearsal ended, someone took Avi to the front row of the Tabernacle, where he sat next to Church officials during the broadcast.

"Mr. Hanani told me, with some emotion, that that was one of his most profound musical experiences as a young man," says Brother McKay. "And then Mr. Hanani asked, 'What can I do for you?' I said that Mayor Teddy Kollek had invited the Tabernacle Choir to come to Israel. Mr. Hanani replied, 'Well, we must have them on Israeli broadcasting.' And I said, 'That's what we're here to discuss.'" This meeting opened the door for the outstanding media support of the Tabernacle Choir's concerts in Israel.[5]

Obviously that usher did not know that the sixteen-year-old music student would one day be in a position to do the Church an immense favor. Nor did the conductor who invited young Mr. Hanani to sit with the choir during rehearsals and see that he had a hospitable place during the performance calculate this kindness, hoping that it would pay off later. They had bread of kindness in their hands and they cast it on the water, instead of hoarding it until it became stale or moldy. And it opened doors.

We've talked about doors and thresholds. We've read several scriptures that describe how doors have opened in miraculous ways. We've seen how it takes human effort to open those doors, even when angels begin the process. We stand on the threshold of adversity and knock on the door with faith.

When Joseph Smith pronounced the benediction of dedication upon the Kirtland Temple, he specifically blessed its threshold. In Doctrine and Covenants, section 109, verses 12–13, we read his prayer:

> . . . That thy glory may rest down upon thy people, and upon this thy house, which we now dedicate to thee, that it may be sanctified and consecrated to be holy, and that thy holy presence may be continually in this house;
>
> And that all people who shall enter upon the threshold of the

Lord's house may feel thy power, and feel constrained to acknowledge that thou hast sanctified it, and that it is thy house, a place of thy holiness.

We are people of the threshold. The people who see our lives as Latter-day Saints are approaching the threshold of the household of faith. Some will enter directly, feeling immediately at home. Others linger on the threshold, unable or unwilling to enter or unknowing of the glories that await them on the other side. We are hosts of the threshold. May our faith reach out to them during these moments on the threshold and lead to the opening of doors.

The very last words that the beloved apostle John recorded in his Revelation was a promise to the Saints who wait for the Savior behind the doors of their own lives. It is in the form of a little dialogue. The Savior says: "Surely I come quickly." And John responds, "Even so, come, Lord Jesus" (Revelation 22:20).

Jesus comes to us in many ways—as comfort at a time of grief, as strength at a time of trial, as kindness from friends when we need help, as sensitivity when our feelings are wounded, as insights when we struggle to understand a principle of the gospel, as whispered answers when we are perplexed with questions.

We wait behind the doors of our own lives. Some of those doors are locked and bolted. Some already stand ajar. Some are heavy and massive, slow to move. Others are almost like curtains or veils, moving with every whisper of the Spirit. May we be alert to the sound of his footstep on our threshold. When he lifts his hand to knock, may our ears catch its first sound. And may we hasten to fling open the door with joy and gratitude, crying, "Even so, come, Lord Jesus."

41

4

COINS: LOST, CAESAR'S, AND CHRIST'S

I'd like to explore the lessons we learn from coins—lost coins, coins that belong to Caesar, and coins that bear Christ's minting—and see how these ideas might apply in our own lives.

Lost Coins

Jesus told the parable of the lost coin:

> Either what woman having ten pieces of silver, if she lose one piece, doth not light a candle, and sweep the house, and seek diligently till she find it?
>
> And when she hath found it, she calleth her friends and her neighbours together, saying, Rejoice with me; for I have found the piece which I had lost.
>
> Likewise, I say unto you, there is joy in the presence of the angels of God over one sinner that repenteth. (Luke 15:8–10)

Jesus told this parable as one of three about lost things. The first was the parable of the lost sheep that had accidentally gone astray, not meaning to leave the flock but not paying attention to where its search for grass was taking it until it had gone out of sight and perhaps gotten itself into a difficulty that made it unable to come back without help. The third parable is the story of the prodigal son, who willfully chose to leave his father's house and then compounded this initial mistake with a series of other mistakes until he had squandered his inheritance, been reduced to fighting with pigs for enough food to keep from starving, and finally looked at his situation and exercised his agency to return to his father's house. And in the middle is the second parable, the parable of the lost coin.

The situation of the coin is different. The coin was passive, inert. It had no agency to exercise; it was not seeking anything when it became lost. In fact, something the woman did must have contributed to its loss. Perhaps she tipped over the jar in which she kept her money and it rolled into a dark corner without her noticing as she gathered up the other nine coins. Perhaps it was lying on the table and the edge of her sleeve brushed it as she went quickly about her duties. Perhaps one of the children saw that it was bright and shiny and took it into a corner to play with. In any case, the coin became separated from the rest of the treasure and was in danger of being overlooked and lost permanently. Fortunately, the woman noticed that it was missing and took the extraordinary action of lighting a candle to illuminate every dark corner; then she swept diligently until the coin tumbled back into visibility. Her attitude was obviously, "As for me and my house, we're going to find this coin!"

Now, in some ways, that may apply to the situation of some Latter-day Saints. You may feel that you're an ordinary coin, just like all the others in your ward and stake, but something happens—an accident, an oversight, insensitivity, carelessness on someone's part, a bitter word, or perhaps even deliberate maliciousness. But something gives you a push away from the other coins. You feel marginalized, ostracized, and shoved to the borders of your group. Maybe gravity or other social forces take over then, and you roll away into a dark corner.

I've talked to dozens of women who have experienced the disorientation and sorrow of becoming single through a husband's death or divorce. And I'm sure that what I have observed applies to single men as well. In most cases, there was very little the woman could have done to prevent this rupture in her marital union, but she still had to deal with the effects. Other members of a ward are not always kind and sensitive. Very seldom do they understand exactly how frightening a divorce or death can be, how debilitating and exhausting sorrow is to bear, even without the extra work of picking up the duties that the spouse once carried and going on alone where once there were two to cheer and encourage each other.

Never-married people often feel equally beset by their single state—blamed for being single, but not sure what they should do about it or what they *could* do about it. When the desires of their heart are righteous, and when their righteous prayers go up to heaven and are seemingly unheard, it is hard to keep on trusting the Lord and his goodness. Sometimes single people blame themselves. Sometimes they express their bewilderment toward the Church that has taught them to prepare for a condition that is denied them. In a Church that teaches so beautifully the doctrine of eternal families, a single person can feel very lost, alone, hidden in a dark corner.

And I have spoken with other dozens of women who have temple marriages, active husbands, and children—blessings for which single sisters sometimes long—but who also feel like lost coins because there are other dimensions of their lives in which they feel inadequate and for which they feel censured, judged, excluded, and rejected.

Something is wrong with this picture. The Savior did not go around making distinctions between individuals. He preached the gospel to all. He healed all. He loved everyone. True, he knew that there were the sinners and the righteous, but he did not turn away the "many publicans and sinners [who] came and sat down with him and his disciples." Instead, he reminded the judgmental Pharisees, "They that be whole need not a physician, but they that are sick" (Matthew 9:10–12). True, he knew about the sheep and goats, wheat and tares, and warned that someday there would come a great separation. But he did not authorize anyone else to make that separation or to cast anyone out before that final judgment came.

And we mustn't cooperate with anyone's efforts to exclude us and leave us out. We're *not* coins. We're not passive and helpless. We don't have to wait for someone to light a candle and start sweeping for us. We can take the steps ourselves that will bring us back with the other coins. I think that a step all of us could and should take, if we haven't already done it, is to know that our lives are acceptable to God, that we are in the right way before him, and that he loves us for who we are.

Perhaps you already have the great peacefulness that comes from this kind of self-acceptance. Or maybe you could have this knowledge if you were willing to ask, but you are afraid of asking. I tell you that you have a right to ask, and I promise you that you will receive light and love and knowledge from our Heavenly Father. Let me tell you a story to illustrate this idea that involved one of our missionaries.

The story began in 1969, not long after my husband, Ed, and I reached Osaka, where Ed had been called to preside over the newly created Japan Okinawa Mission and where I was president of the women's auxiliaries. But I didn't learn the rest of the story until after Ed's death. Jim Renell of Boise, Idaho, attended our missionary reunion in July 1993, the first reunion we held without Ed, who had died in March. The next month, he wrote to me, sharing a special moment that he had had with my husband. His letter reads:

> On August 17, 1969, transfers had just come out and new senior companions were made. I was transferred [but] . . . had not been made senior. I wrote to the president about my dismay. . . . I cherish his response even today. His kind rebuke was evident in the note as was his love. What a learning moment I received! I recognized it and kept it all these years for that reason.

He enclosed a copy of the letter Ed had tapped out on the type-writer in his own self-taught, two-fingered, hunt-and-peck typing:

Thank you for writing me. . . . I can understand your disap-pointment and I am sorry this is the way I was inspired to make the transfers. . . . I don't think you should think . . . you were "passed by" or that you were not good enough or that someone in authority over you did not feel that you were [not] capable or prepared enough. If you do, you only hurt yourself and you bog yourself down. . . . You must have trust in the leaders. . . . I personally feel that you are doing a good job, have a good attitude, and I feel you are ready to be called as Senior Companion. However, I was not inspired to call you to be Sr. on this transfer.

I hope this explanation helps. I appreciate your expressing your feelings to me. Thanks for sustaining me. I hope you don't stay discouraged too long because if you do, you only hurt yourself. Lord bless you always. Keep up your good work. Sincerely yours, Pres. O

I didn't know about this particular transfer or about Elder Renell's feelings of disappointment, but the letter was altogether typical of Ed. He did not scold the missionary or blame him for his feelings. Ed told him honestly that he was not inspired to call him to be senior even though Ed felt he was ready and qualified to be senior. It is evident, from what Ed says, that if Ed alone had been making the decision, Elder Renell would have been a senior com-panion. In a way, Ed was saying, "I'm puzzled too, Elder. I don't understand this either."

Then Ed looked beyond the moment to teach Elder Renell a lesson about trusting his leaders and focusing on the service, rather than the position. That was a lesson Ed had learned thor-oughly. It was very important to him, and Elder Renell, who was made a senior companion soon afterward, continued with his letter, explaining why Ed's message was so important to him that he wanted to share it with me:

> Several years ago I was a bishopric counselor—a position I had held several times in different cities. I enjoyed the position and felt that I was serving as I should. Abruptly both the other counselor and I were released. The counselor had asked to be released because he was retiring and wished to travel. I had not. It came as a complete surprise to me. I felt numb. In my concern I remembered and re-read this note from President Okazaki that I had kept from so many years before. The message was still clear. It made sense. I knew it was right.
>
> Several months later I found out that the stake was splitting with changes in boundaries reshaping our ward. Both the other counselor and I were in a different ward than the standing bishop. He had been instructed to select counselors from a specific geographic area without having to explain in order to keep turmoil at a minimum prior to the official announcement. What a difference it made to me to have my mission president's counsel from years before, and to read it again! What a difference it made to my family and to other ward members to see the way I chose to react! President Okazaki had spoken to me again from across the years with wise counsel.

Elder Renell could have become a lost coin on his mission. How grateful Ed must have been that Elder Renell felt he could write to him, could be honest about his hurt feelings, and could ask for an explanation. How grateful I am that Elder Renell had the spiritual maturity to hear Ed's explanation in the spirit in which it was meant—to feel Ed's love and to accept the workings of the Spirit even when he didn't understand them. I think there are puzzling things in everybody's life, when we can't understand what the Lord is telling us or when we can't understand why or how it comes in the form that it does. At times like that, it's okay to ask questions. It's okay to say, "Tell me why." Our part is to trust that there is an answer, even if we can't hear it or don't recognize the answer that we want in it.

There was a third part of Elder Renell's letter—a part that explained why he trusted Ed enough to ask him a potentially embarrassing question like, "Why didn't you make me a senior?" and why Ed trusted him enough to tell him the truth. Elder Renell wrote:

> Another incident that will always burn brightly in my heart is the three-day tanjobi taikai [a conference to celebrate the mission's birthday] that ended September 10, 1969. On the first morning's meeting on September 8th, President Okazaki stood before all missionaries assembled for the very first time together in one place. He beamed his ever-present smile and energetically greeted us with "ohayo gozaimasu!!!"—to which every missionary responded in unison.
>
> My dearest Sister O., as long as I live, I will never forget his reaction . . . or yours on seeing his. Tears welled in his eyes and the words he was in the midst of saying caught in his throat as he stood before all his missionaries. The love shown by his spontaneous reaction will never, ever leave me. We all felt it. I relive it again as I write this.

Ed loved our missionaries with his whole heart. I so appreciate Elder Renell sharing both parts of the experience with me, including this last little vignette of Ed, overcome by the love of the missionaries. Do you know that feeling? Have you been speaking to someone when a wave of love so strong has swept over you, preventing you from uttering another word? I don't know what Ed wanted to say, but I do know that what he communicated in that silent moment when emotion choked him was more important than any words he could have uttered.

I'm so glad that Elder Renell did not become a lost coin in the mission field, or later during a moment of hurt and disappointment, because the one element that all of the parables of loss have in common is rejoicing at the finding. The shepherd, bringing back the lost sheep, called his friends to rejoice with him. The woman called her friends and neighbors together, saying, "Rejoice with me" (Luke 15:9). And the father of the prodigal son ordered a feast and merrymaking to mark the return of his lost son. Remember that rejoicing if there are moments when you feel lost, estranged, and pushed out to the margins of your ward or stake. You are never on the margins of the Father's love. You are always in his heart and in his hands.

Caesar's Coins

The second incident involving coinage that I want to discuss is the story of the Pharisees and Sadducees trying to trap Jesus into speaking against the Roman tax. Matthew records:

> And they sent out unto him their disciples with the Herodians, saying, Master, we know that thou art true, and teachest the way of God in truth, neither carest thou for any man: for thou regardest not the person of men.
>
> Tell us therefore, What thinkest thou? Is it lawful to give tribute unto Caesar, or not?
>
> But Jesus perceived their wickedness, and said, Why tempt ye me, ye hypocrites?
>
> Shew me the tribute money. And they brought unto him a penny.
>
> And he saith unto them, Whose is this image and superscription?
>
> They say unto him, Caesar's. Then saith he unto them, Render therefore unto Caesar the things which are Caesar's; and unto God the things that are God's.
>
> When they had heard these words, they marvelled, and left him, and went their way. (Matthew 22:16–22)

We live in Caesar's world. Very few of us are in circumstances where we can count ourselves exempt from Adam and Eve's lot of

49

earning their bread by the sweat of their brow. And I'm not sure that it would be much of a blessing if we could! The few episodes of daytime television I've seen seem to have main characters who are in deep trouble that they mostly cause for themselves because they have too much spare time. If they had to put in eight hours on the job, their lives would become much less complicated overnight.

Under ideal circumstances, the Church tells us, children need a full-time mother at home with them. We all know that principle and know that it's a correct principle. But the Church can't create ideal circumstances for everyone. We each have to deal with the realities of our lives, and one of those realities is that we have to do what it takes to take care of ourselves and of those who need it—the young, the old, the sick, and the disabled.

Let's not get Caesar's world mixed up with God's world. Sometimes people have told me that they expect the Church or the bishop to take care of them because they're living the gospel. That's not a correct expectation. The Church and the bishop are there to give a hand when the load gets too heavy, but our job is to carry as much of that load as we possibly can by ourselves and to grow stronger so that we can shoulder more of it.

When Ed and I were growing up in Hawaii, we knew that our families weren't wealthy in anything except good values. Ed's father died before he was out of high school. We knew we were going to have to work hard to get educations and then work hard at our professions to get ahead. And we did. We've been financially independent all our married lives, even when times were very hard.

Ironically, one of the hardest times was right after we came back from our mission. Ed had quit his job to serve as a mission president and didn't have another one. Thanks to a very astute principal who had seen that I applied for a leave of absence instead of resigning when I left, I had my job teaching second grade waiting for me. Our oldest son entered BYU just a few weeks after we returned. The people to whom we had rented our house had left, so we could move right back in, but our luggage went astray and meandered all over the South Pacific before it caught up with us. We had only my paycheck to live from, and we had to be very frugal. After we'd bought the boys a bare minimum of school clothes, there was virtually nothing left, so Ed and I wore the summer clothes that were in our single suitcase until the end of November. A very thoughtful sister in the ward, as the weather got colder and colder, noticed my light, summery dress and asked tactfully about it.

"Oh, we're just waiting for our luggage to get home," I said cheerfully.

She didn't say anything more at the time, but appeared at our door the next day with several warm dresses, sweaters, and skirts from her own closet, explaining, "I really don't wear these anymore, and it would be such a kindness to me if you'd use them." Well, I knew who was being kind, and many heartfelt prayers went up in thanksgiving for Louise Mugleston Thacker and her generous heart.

These months were especially hard on Ed because he felt so keenly his responsibility to support the family. He looked everywhere for a job in his field, which was social work—but there were very few openings. He didn't stop there, though. He followed up every lead that he heard about, signed up with agencies, and faithfully tracked down want ads in the newspaper.

It was a very difficult autumn. Ed had worked hard to rise out of the laboring class, but he was not too proud to take a job in unskilled labor to work for us. I felt such pride in him when he determinedly went off to apply for a job as a warehouse worker, but he came back disappointed. The foreman looked at his résumé, shook his head, and said: "You're overqualified. You won't stay here long."

I remember that Ed also applied for a social work job at Catholic Charities. The person who was interviewing him looked at his résumé and said, "I see that you've been working for your church for the last three years as a mission president. What were you doing there?" Ed explained what a mission president did— and it was obvious that the job of mission president required a lot of ability. The interviewer looked shocked and said, "How come your church doesn't help you out? You'd think the least they could do is help you find a job after you've worked for them for three years. Why have they left you stranded like this?"

Even our boys struggled to understand and accept it. "Goll, Dad," I remember Bob, who was a senior in high school, saying, "you've given the Lord three years of your time. You were a good mission president. You worked hard. We're all trying to live the gospel. Why won't the Lord help you?"

To all of these questions, Ed gave the same answer: "That wasn't part of the deal." He understood that Caesar's world runs by Caesar's rules and that the Lord seldom intervenes. Bad things happen to righteous people. They get sick, lose jobs, and have problems. The Lord doesn't bargain or make deals. Even a total commitment to the Lord's work doesn't mean that you can drive a car without gasoline, not pay the mortgage, and not owe taxes. It's not part of the deal.

We kept praying, of course, and Ed worked at whatever he could find until finally an opening came for a social worker in February, six months after we returned home. Ed was very successful at his job. When he retired, he was director of his department and had initiated several new programs. But I don't think I was ever prouder of him than I was when he humbly and willingly applied to be a warehouseman, answering in faith that material security "wasn't part of the deal" when he had accepted a calling to be mission president.

We await with faith and anticipation the time when Christ will come again, in glory through the skies, when every knee will bow and every tongue confess that he is the Christ. But he has not yet returned except in quiet, private visits, as when he appeared to Joseph Smith. Jesus is the King of kings and Lord of lords, but he was born a helpless baby in Bethlehem, just another child born to poverty-stricken parents in Caesar's world.

Angels intervened to save his life, so that Joseph, Mary, and the babe were on the road to Egypt when Herod's soldiers swept through, stabbing and trampling the baby boys of the town. But angels did not intervene to find a safer or more comfortable place for Mary to give birth in than a humble stable. It was Caesar's world, and private bedchambers were to be had only with money.

I don't imagine that many of us need a reminder that we live in Caesar's world. But if you have prayed about your economic future and felt promptings to take certain steps, I hope you have been obedient to that direction, for your sake and for the sake of your family. In Caesar's world, your temporal well-being must be purchased with Caesar's coin, not with God's.

Now, having said this, I remind you that there are still angels, and there are still miracles. Pray for them, seek for them, and live worthy of them. When the tax collectors came, demanding tribute of the Savior, Jesus sent Peter to the sea with a fish hook and told him to "take up the fish that first cometh up; and when thou hast opened his mouth, thou shalt find a piece of money: that take, and give unto them for me and thee" (Matthew 17:27).

Christ's Coins

We've talked about lost coins and about Caesar's coins. Now let's talk about Christ's coins. When Alma the Younger resigned from the chief judgeship and began his great preaching mission in the land of Zarahemla, he used a metaphor that reminds me of the minting of coins. He reminded his backsliding people that his own father, Alma, "believe[d] in the words which were delivered by the mouth of Abinadi . . . And according to his faith there was a mighty change wrought in his heart." He then preached this message to his people at the Waters of Mormon, the parents of the people to whom he was then speaking: "And behold," Alma said, " . . . a mighty change was also wrought in *their* hearts, and they humbled themselves and put their trust in the true and living God." Then Alma asked this piercing question: "And now behold,

I ask of you, my brethren [and sisters] of the church, have ye spiritually been born of God? Have ye received his image in your countenances? Have ye experienced this mighty change in your hearts?"

He asked a series of questions about exactly what such a change would mean: it would mean faith in the redemption of Christ, a belief in the Atonement and the resurrection, and the reality of accountability for how they used their agency. "Can ye look up to God at that day with a pure heart and clean hands?" Alma asked. "I say unto you, can you look up, having the image of God engraven upon your countenances?" (Alma 5:11–19; emphasis added).

It's worth reading the entire chapter of Alma 5 when you have time, I think, and putting yourself in the position of those people to whom Alma was bearing his testimony. And then also turn to Mosiah chapter 5 and read the response of the people after King Benjamin had implored them so powerfully to come unto Christ.

> He sent among them, desiring to know of his people if they believed the words which he had spoken unto them.
>
> And they all cried with one voice, saying: Yea, we believe all the words which thou hast spoken unto us; and also, we know of their surety and truth, because of the Spirit of the Lord Omnipotent, which has wrought a mighty change in us, or in our hearts, that we have no more disposition to do evil, but to do good continually.
>
> And we, ourselves, also, through the infinite goodness of God, and the manifestations of his Spirit, have great views of that which is to come; and were it expedient, we could prophesy of all things.
>
> And it is the faith which we have had on the things which our king has spoken unto us that has brought us to this great knowledge, whereby we do rejoice with such exceedingly great joy.
>
> And we are willing to enter into a covenant with our God to

do his will, and to be obedient to his commandments in all things that he shall command us, all the remainder of our days, that we may not bring upon ourselves a never-ending torment, as has been spoken by the angel, that we may not drink out of the cup of the wrath of God.

And now, these are the words which king Benjamin desired of them; and therefore he said unto them: Ye have spoken the words that I desired; and the covenant which ye have made is a righteous covenant.

And now, because of the covenant which ye have made ye shall be called the children of Christ, his sons, and his daughters; for behold, this day he hath spiritually begotten you; for ye say that your hearts are changed through faith on his name; therefore, ye are born of him and have become his sons and his daughters.

In other words, they had spiritually received his image in their countenances and had willingly taken his name upon them to begin the transforming work of becoming Christians. King Benjamin continued:

And under this head ye are made free, and there is no other head whereby ye can be made free. There is no other name given whereby salvation cometh; therefore, I would that ye should take upon you the name of Christ, all you that have entered into the covenant with God that ye should be obedient unto the end of your lives. (Mosiah 5:1–8)

How, then, do we become Christ's coins? By experiencing a mighty change of heart and by receiving the impress of his Spirit. Alma suggests, and I believe it's true, that you can somehow see the countenance of our Savior in the countenance of a true Christian. And as King Benjamin reminds us, our choice to become Christians is not a matter of saying a few words or signing a piece of paper or going to a certain set of meetings on Sundays. It involves a change of heart. We must choose to become Christ's. We must choose it freely. We must choose obedience to his way. Loren Seibold, a religious writer, makes this point strongly:

> God can place His imprint on anything He wants to—except for one thing: you.
>
> You're the only part of His creation that doesn't have to accept it. You've got a choice. You can say, "No, God. I don't want to wear Your mark."
>
> This is perhaps the most important question you'll ever have to answer: With whose image are you imprinted? whose inscription is on you?
>
> You see, you will bear the imprint of whatever you make most important in your life. And that image can obliterate the image God intends you to bear. Do you love success more than you love the Lord? The world will be more than happy to stamp you with the image of success. Or perhaps you prefer self-indulgence? Or lust?
>
> But what if God's image has already disappeared from your life? God sent His son, Jesus Christ, expressly to deal to that situation. His mission, in part, is to remint the human coinage of the world.
>
> Coins are minted in fire. Sometimes Christ must use a pretty hot fire to remint us, to renew His image on our lives. He may have to use the fire of grief or the fire of loss. Or it may take the fire of introspection for us to see ourselves as we really are so that we become willing to accept His image.[1]

Sometimes *burning* is not too strong a word for the feelings we have. We all have experienced pangs of remorse that have scorched like fire as we have contemplated with anguish deeds we wish undone or words we wish unsaid. The Lord can deal with such fiery pangs. His grace and mercy are like the gentle dews of heaven, quenching the fires of remorse and reviving our scorched consciences. But he has fires of his own to kindle in our souls.

We talk about a burning conviction when our testimonies are strong. Jeremiah talked about the word of God being "in mine heart as a burning fire shut up in my bones" (Jeremiah 20:9). We can warm and strengthen others with the warmth of our own faith. The radiance of Christ, who is the light of the world, can shine in even the darkest places.

Christ came among us quietly, speaking his words among us so that they would find their own way to our hearts. He spoke of lost coins, and of rejoicings when they were found. He himself is the good shepherd who will stand at the door of the sheepfold to welcome us all home.

Remember to give Caesar the homage that is due to Caesar in this world, but give Caesar no more. Caesar's coin is not coin of the realm in God's world. Remember the humility of a returned mission president looking for a job, trusting in the Lord, and saying with trust and faith, "That wasn't part of the deal."

The fires of adversity and also the burnings of the Holy Ghost will pass over each one of us. Counterfeit coins cannot withstand the everlasting burnings in which the righteous will dwell, but when we have received the image of Christ in our countenances and in our hearts, then we know we cannot be satisfied with counterfeits.

Our Heavenly Father sent us into the world with his image in each countenance. Each of us is on a quest in this life to purify ourselves of mists and veils so that we may see truly and clearly into each other's hearts and there perceive that each one is a sister or a brother, equally a beloved child of our loving Heavenly Parents. When the joyous day comes that we are called to stand before our Savior and our Father, may we all look up with the image of God in our countenances, not counterfeit, but pure and loyal through and through.

FREE TO CHOOSE

President David O. McKay taught: "Next to the bestowal of life itself, the right to direct that life is God's greatest gift to man. . . . Freedom of choice is more to be treasured than any possession earth can give."[1] This puts me in mind of a wonderful story I heard about President Gordon B. Hinckley.

> While chairing a budget session held early one afternoon in which Church Educational System managers were presenting their budget needs for the coming year, feelings became intense. Another General Authority turned to President Hinckley and asked, "What do *you* think?" President Hinckley, who had been listening with his chin resting on the palms of his hands, replied: "I think I am never again going to have stuffed pork chops for lunch."[2]

As you can imagine, that broke the tension in the room and after a good laugh, they were all able to discuss the budget problem with a fresh perspective.

Well, the choice to avoid stuffed pork chops is probably not an earth-shattering one, but sometimes the ability to make decisions and the range of choices available is frightening to us. We think, "But what if I make a mistake? What if I make the wrong choice?"

Mahatma Gandhi pointed out a simple truth: "Freedom is not worth having if it does not connote freedom to err."[3]

Did our Heavenly Father know we were going to make mistakes when we came to the earth? Yes, he did. Did he know that we wouldn't always have enough information to choose between two good alternatives? Yes, he did. Did he suspect that sometimes our emotions would get in the way of clear thinking and that we'd make a hasty decision that we'd later regret? Yes, of course he knew that. Furthermore, he knew that it wasn't just mistakes that would occur. He knew that we would use our agency unwisely, incorrectly, even perversely so that we weren't just choosing between two good alternatives but between good and evil, and that sometimes we would choose evil.

Do you know what? He planned a world in which that would be possible, and we accepted this plan in the premortal existence with shouts of joy and rejoicing, pledging ourselves to accept Jesus Christ as our Savior so that we could repent and have our mistakes wiped out and be forgiven for our sins. Trying for a system in which people never made mistakes was not our Heavenly Father's way. That was Satan's way. He's the one who wanted to eliminate mistakes and sins, but the way he wanted to do it was by eliminating choice. What happens to people who have never had choices and then suddenly get to make them? Are they equipped to discern wisely between truth and error? Might sin seem extra enticing to someone who has never been tempted before? I think so.

Our Heavenly Father wants to eliminate sins too, but he wants to do it the riskier, longer, more complicated way of teaching us correct principles, letting us learn from our own experiences, experiencing joy when we make good decisions and sorrow when we make bad decisions, accepting the atonement of the Savior with real gratitude because we need him so much, and learning to follow him out of love and faith. Yes, not everyone will do it. But at the end of this process, our Heavenly Parents will have sons and daughters who are their peers, their friends, and their colleagues.

We also will be gods. We will be able to love perfectly, like them. We will be able to choose right freely, like them. We will prize and cherish and never infringe on the agency of others, like them. In other words, we will be able to be trusted with the powers of a god because we will have acquired the perfect love and self-control and attributes of a god.

I was inspired by the story of David Meilsoe, a nineteen-year-old member of the Church in Denmark, who plays on that country's championship basketball team—but never on Sunday. Now he is planning to serve a mission. "Many people my age have not yet made any major decisions concerning their lives," he said. "But there comes a time when making a decision is necessary, and . . . I have made the right decision."[4]

Does that tell us something about raising our children? Does that tell us that they need the freedom to make their own choices, maybe even when we think they're not quite ready? And can we be prepared to provide information and share our own perspective but love them enough to step back and give them free choice?

And does it say something to us in the decisions we must make? Sometimes we spend more time looking for someone to tell us what to do than we do making the decision itself. We need to exercise choices. We need to be wise. We need to collect information, consult our own needs and desires, consult others who are involved in that decision, and seek the spirit of the Lord. And then we need to decide! And after we've made a choice and lived with the consequences of that choice for a while, then perhaps we need to modify the first choice or make another choice. That's fine! Our Heavenly Father granted our agency so that we could choose and choose and choose again. And we hope, with each choice, that we're becoming more like Jesus. In darkness there is no choice. It is light that enables us to see the differences between things, and it is Christ who gives us light.

Remember the great sermon of Lehi near the end of his life, a sermon in which he distilled the most essential knowledge about the principles of the gospel, which he had garnered throughout a lifetime of following the Lord and seeking to understand his ways. He was speaking to his sons, but I'm paraphrasing it slightly so that his words apply directly to us:

> And the Messiah cometh in the fulness of time, that he may redeem . . . [us] from the fall. And because . . . [we] are redeemed from the fall [we] have become free forever, knowing good from evil; to act for [our]selves and not to be acted upon, save it be by the punishment of the law at the great and last day, according to the commandments which God hath given.
>
> Wherefore, [we] are free according to the flesh; and all things are given [us] which are expedient. . . . And [we] are free to choose liberty and eternal life, through the great Mediator of all . . . or to choose captivity and death, according to the captivity and power of the devil; for he seeketh that all . . . might be miserable like unto himself.
>
> And now . . . I would that ye should look to the great Mediator, and hearken unto his great commandments; and be faithful unto his words, and choose eternal life, according to the will of his Holy Spirit. (2 Nephi 2:26–28)

Choosing to Be Temple Worthy

One of my favorite stories about President Howard W. Hunter is the tale of his eightieth birthday celebration. His family congregated at his home and his two daughters-in-law set his dining room table with elegant china, crystal, and silver.

> After dinner the family sat around the table and took turns telling [President Hunter] what they most admired about him and how he had influenced their lives. It was, according to [one of his daughters-in-law], a tender time, with many tears shed. Then someone said, "Tell us, Grandpa, what you think we should know—what advice do you have for our lives." After a

brief pause, . . . President Hunter replied solemnly, "Well, when you take a shower, keep the curtains inside the tub."[5]

I'd say that's very good advice. And when we make that choice, we'll reap the reward of not having to mop up the bathroom afterwards. I'd also suggest that we pay very close attention to President Hunter's additional advice regarding our choices. He has asked us to be a "temple-attending and temple-loving people," and has invited us:

> Let us hasten to the temple as frequently as time and means and personal circumstances allow. Let us go not only for our kindred dead, but let us also go for the personal blessings of temple worship, for the sanctity and safety which is provided within those hallowed and consecrated walls. The temple is a place of beauty, it is a place of revelation, it is a place of peace. It is the house of the Lord. It is holy unto the Lord. It should be holy unto us.[6]

What benefits do we reap from choosing to accept this invitation of President Hunter? I think there is a great hunger for holiness in all of us, a great desire to be close to God, to feel the peace of a quiet conscience, and confidence that we can receive revelation for the problems and difficulties that perplex us. President Hunter issued his invitation in terms that are accessible to any member of the Church anywhere. For someone who is worthy of a temple recommend, no matter where in the world he or she may be, the same blessings are available: a quiet conscience, internal peace, closeness to God, and a right to personal revelation.

President Hunter spoke again on the blessings of the temple on a warm June afternoon when he was visiting the site of the Nauvoo Temple in connection with the 150th anniversary of the martyrdom of Joseph and Hyrum Smith. He said: "As you know, earlier this month I began my ministry by expressing a deep desire to have more and more Church members become temple worthy.

As in Joseph's day, having worthy and endowed members is the key to building the kingdom in all the world. Temple worthiness ensures that our lives are in harmony with the will of the Lord, and we are attuned to receive His guidance in our lives."[7]

I've always felt that going to the temple is going to the house of the Lord—like the house of a friend where the parents have just stepped out for a moment. But the children are there—being sure that the lights are on, the rooms are dusted and cleaned, that everything is in perfect order for when the parents return—and so happy to be there and to welcome us there, too. I love the sense of glad anticipation just before a session begins. I hope you love the temple and go there often, or that you will have that opportunity more frequently as your family gets older and as your circumstances change. But the wonderful, gracious, kindly aspect of President Hunter's message is that he invites us to be worthy of the temple, whether we can attend often or not. He knows that we can find peace in righteousness no matter where we are.

Choosing to Serve

Another favorite story of mine is from the life of President Thomas S. Monson. Hanging across from President Monson's desk where he can see it when he glances up is a painting of the Savior, which he has had ever since he was a twenty-two-year-old bishop. He says: "I have tried to pattern my life after the Master. . . . Whenever I have had a difficult decision to make, or perhaps have had to measure the request to give a blessing against the endless demands of some of my paperwork, I have always looked at that picture and asked myself, 'What would He do?' Then I try to do it.'" Then he smiles and adds, "The choice has never been to stay and do paperwork!"[8]

My dear brothers and sisters, sometimes we get confused between our jobs and our work. President Monson's job was obviously to do the paperwork, managing the very important administrative tasks that keep the Church functioning smoothly. But his work was the work of Christ: to be among the people, drying here the tears of a widow bereaved of her only child, there being a guest at the feast, or touching the eyes of a blind man. All of us have the same work to do—the work of doing good to others. Paul wrote to the Galatians: "By love serve one another. For all the law is fulfilled in one word, even in this; Thou shalt love thy neighbour as thyself" (Galatians 5:13–14).

A friend of mine, Launie Severinsen, has written a poem entitled "Alternative," describing how we need to focus on our work instead of our jobs:

> With hobnail boots in fine repair
> We go forth every day—
> Treading down the tender hearts
> Of those who pass our way.
>
> . . .
>
> [Christ] walked forth daily sandal-shod,
> Comforting those who grieved,
> Aware of all who suffered pain—
> He blessed all who received.
> Offering His eternal love,
> Freely, day to day,
> He gently walked among mankind,
> Showing the better way.
> Should we then, in boots hobnailed,
> Continue as we choose?
> Or can we find a way, more fine,
> With sandals for our shoes.[9]

And perhaps, when it comes to human hearts, we should move among them barefoot, so that we can feel the press of pebbles, even small ones, and the grateful coolness of tender grass. This is an invitation to kindness we can all accept. As Henri F. Amiel said, "Life is short and we have not too much time for gladdening the hearts of those who are traveling the dark way with us. Oh, be swift to love! Make haste to be kind!"[10]

Think again of President Monson. There were eighty-seven widows in his ward when he was a young bishop. He continued to visit them to the end of their lives. A lifelong friend commented:

> When the rest of us were released as bishops, we just kind of moved on to the next task and left the widows to our successors. Not Tom. He somehow found time to keep visiting them. He is the most loyal man I know. . . .
>
> One night during the Christmas holidays some years ago, President Monson was making his customary rounds to "his" widows, leaving gifts purchased from his own pocket, including plump dressed chickens that were, in the early years, raised in his own coops. In one . . . rest [home] . . . he found one of his ward members, alone and silent in the darkened room of a world made even darker by the onset of blindness. As President Monson made his way to this sweet sister's side, she reached out awkwardly, groping for the hand of the only visitor she had received in the whole of the Christmas season. . . . "Oh, Bishop," she wept . . . "I knew *you* would come."[11]

Let me tell you two more stories about people who chose kindness, both anonymous accounts. The first one is by a young man who says:

> When I was in college, I worked part-time at a sporting goods store. There was a kid who would come by two or three times a week to visit with this baseball mitt that he wanted to buy. My manager and I would joke about him not only because he was so dedicated and persistent, but also because he had picked the best and most expensive mitt in the shop to get obsessed about.
>
> This went on for months. The kid would come in, and you could tell he was so relieved that the mitt was still there. He

would put it on, pound his fist into the pocket a couple of times, and then very carefully put it back onto the shelf and leave. Finally, one day he came in with a shoe box and a smile about eight miles wide and announced that he wanted to buy the mitt. So the manager brought the mitt over to the cash register while the kid counted out a shoe box worth of nickels, quarters, and dimes. His stash came to exactly $19.98. The mitt cost $79.98, not including tax. My manager looked at the price tag, and sure enough the 7 was a little smudged, enough that a desperately hopeful seven-year-old could imagine it to be a 1. Then he looked at me, smiled, and very carefully recounted. "Yep, exactly $19.98." Wrapping up the mitt, he gave it to the boy.[12]

This choice involved some financial sacrifice, but what it gave in return was an enormous and secret source of pleasure that has lasted that young clerk's lifetime. That pleasure is part of Christ's own love, spilling over and manifested through the love and care of that sporting goods store owner. The clerk didn't perform the act. He stood by and observed it, but that was enough to fill him with the same spilling-over joy that kindness brings.

The second story is from a woman and is something we can all relate to:

There was a time in my life, when everything was working so smoothly, I found myself sitting at home one Saturday with all my work done, all my household chores completed: dishes washed, laundry folded and put away, house dusted, grocery shopping completed, and that delicious feeling of having nothing to do. Then I thought about a friend from work who was a single mother of two small children and never seemed to have the time for anything. I jumped into my car, drove over to her house, walked in and said, "Put me to work." At first she didn't really believe it, but we ended up having a great time, cleaning like mad, taking time out to feed and play with the kids, and then diving back into the chores.[13]

Now, this woman had worked hard on her own projects. She could have chosen to reward herself with a leisurely afternoon of sitting in the backyard with a glass of lemonade and a good book. And that would have been a memorable afternoon. But obviously she never forgot the pleasure of spending the afternoon "cleaning like mad" in someone else's house.

The nature of mortality is that we always have to make choices. Sometimes the choices are between good and evil. Those choices are relatively simple. But frequently we have to make choices between things that are both good. These choices are harder to make. Even though we may never know that we have made the best choice between two good things that compete for our time and attention, I know that our hearts will not reproach us if we consistently make choices that will enable us to show kindness to another brother or sister. I pray that we may be fellow-laborers with the Savior in our true work—to love one another as the Savior has loved us.

A DISCIPLE'S HEART

Esther's tale is one of the most wonderfully told stories in the Old Testament because it has so much tension and suspense in it. First, there's the suspense of wondering whether Esther will be selected above all the other eligible maidens to become queen. And then there's the anger of Haman against the noble and patriotic Mordecai, Esther's uncle, which he generalizes into a desire to annihilate all of Mordecai's people. And the only way that seems possible to stop him is to pit this young and beautiful but politically inexperienced girl against the wily Haman in a contest of wits to influence the king.

Esther points out to her uncle that she may be completely unsuccessful. The king hasn't sent for her for thirty days, and it's death to come into his presence uninvited unless he holds out the golden scepter. Isn't this taking a terrible chance?

Mordecai responds, not with comforting half-truths or with pretty, reassuring lies, but with the truth, the whole truth, and nothing but the truth: "Think not with thyself that thou shalt escape in the king's house, more than all the Jews. For if thou altogether holdest thy peace at this time, then shall there enlargement and deliverance arise to the Jews from another place; but thou and thy father's house shall be destroyed." And then he offers her the hopeful message: "And who knoweth whether thou art come to the kingdom for such a time as this?" (Esther 4:13–14).

Well, you know how the story turned out. The king held out his scepter to Esther, she engaged his interest on behalf of her people, Haman was hanged on the very gibbet that he'd erected for Mordecai, and the Jews received royal permission to plunder and slaughter their enemies instead of the other way around. I suppose that's a happy ending. It's certainly a symmetrical ending, even though I think it lacks something in the department of higher ethics.

But let's focus on that key phrase, "for such a time as this." What is our time? Unquestionably it is a time of challenge, adversity, and trial. There has never been a time when conditions were otherwise, except perhaps in the city of Enoch and among the Nephites in the years after the Savior's ministry. I'm not very interested in focusing on drugs, gangs, materialism, violence, pollution, and other problems. I'm more interested in our response to these problems. We live in fearful times. Do we let them make us afraid?

Esther must have felt very safe, in some respects, when the doors of the house of women closed behind her. She would never again have to worry about being run down in the marketplace or wonder where her next meal was coming from. But when Mordecai pointed out that the edict of annihilation would not stop at the gates of the palace, then those tall, protecting doors must have felt like a trap. She could have wept or tried to escape in drink or tried to deny it. But escape and denial are the responses of fear, not faith.

Her choice was to respond with faith. She called a three-day fast of the Jews in the city, in which she and her maidens joined, while she prepared her heart and her spirit to break the law of the kingdom. Clearly she knew what the consequences might be, for she said, "And if I perish, I perish" (Esther 4:16). This is a dramatic moment—the moment of commitment. Isn't there a little tingle of excitement in reading those words of courage and decision? She was willing to risk her life for this cause.

But of course, if we stop to think about it, we can see that she was not saying anything dramatic or brave at all. She was saying no more than the literal truth. She was a mortal woman. Death would come inevitably for her, as it does for everyone. If she failed to win the king's heart and turn away the edict, she would die within a few weeks. If she succeeded and the king granted her petition, she would survive the threatened date of slaughter—but she would still die someday. Her only real choice was *how* she would live and what cause she would give herself to before she died.

This is the choice we all have. What cause will we commit ourselves to? How will we choose to live, even in fearsome times?

This choice was never more eloquently expressed, in my opinion, than in words that playwright Maxwell Anderson puts in the mouth of Joan of Arc as she waits in prison on the night before she is to be executed. When an accuser taunts her with being arrogant in seeking martyrdom, as though she were some favored pet of God's, she answers with the utmost simplicity: "Every man gives his life for what he believes. Every woman gives her life for what she believes. Sometimes people believe in little or nothing, nevertheless they give up their lives to that little or nothing. One life is all we have, and we live it as we believe in living it, and then it's gone. But to surrender what you are, and live without belief—that's more terrible than dying—more terrible than dying young."[1]

We find ourselves in troubled and troubling times. We desire a sanctuary, a city of refuge, a safe place where we can hide with our children. My message to you is that no place is safe unless we are strong enough to defend it, and that our strength, our shield, and our defense must be in our individual testimonies of the Savior.

We must develop a disciple's heart. Only in such a way can we have the internal strength to meet the challenges of our day with faith and courage, instead of with fear and faltering.

Another biblical figure who showed faith in the face of

tremendous challenges was Job. When the Lord invited Satan to consider his servant Job, he said, "There is none like him in the earth." What trait did he single out as Job's most important characteristic? His integrity. "He holdeth fast his integrity," even though all of his possessions and his family were destroyed (Job 2:3). The Old Testament also records the Lord's counsel to Solomon, to "walk before me, as David thy father walked, in integrity of heart" (1 Kings 9:4). Since we know that David was not free from grievous sins, it is a great comfort to me to realize that the Lord accepted him in his weakness and looked upon the steadfastness of his heart. That same beautiful phrase, "integrity of heart," appears twice in the Doctrine and Covenants, praising modern Saints for their commitment: "Blessed is my servant Hyrum Smith; for I, the Lord, love him because of the integrity of his heart, and because he loveth that which is right before me, saith the Lord" (D&C 124:15). And the second occurrence: "And again, verily I say unto you, my servant George Miller is without guile; he may be trusted because of the integrity of his heart; and for the love which he has to my testimony I, the Lord, love him" (D&C 124:20).

Think what it would mean to hear the voice of the Lord saying, "And I say unto you, my servant Mary, or my servant Deborah, or my servant Susan, I, the Lord, love her because of the integrity of her heart." How can we aspire to this wonderful condition—to integrity of heart?

I believe there is only one way. We must give our hearts to the Savior so that he becomes the light of our lives and the touchstone by which we measure every relationship, every action, every word, and every thought, whether it is worthy of him or not. President Ezra Taft Benson said:

As members of The Church of Jesus Christ of Latter-day Saints, we need to place unreserved confidence in the Lord Jesus Christ, whom we accept as the Son of God. Until the world accepts Him as the Savior of mankind, lives His teachings, and looks to Him as the *Way*, the *Truth*, and the *Life* in all phases of our lives, we shall continue in our anxiety about the future and our ability to cope with the challenges that mortality brings to each of us.

The fundamental principle of our religion is faith in the Lord Jesus Christ. Why is it expedient that we center our confidence, our hope, and our trust in one solitary figure? Why is faith in Him so necessary to peace of mind in this life and hope in the world to come?

Our answers to these questions determine whether we face the future with courage, hope, and optimism or with apprehension, anxiety, and pessimism.

My message and testimony is this: Only Jesus Christ is uniquely qualified to provide that hope, that confidence, and that strength we need to overcome the world and rise above our human failings. To do so, we must place our faith in Him and live by His laws and teachings.[2]

The Lord counseled in Doctrine and Covenants 124:45: "And if my people will hearken unto my voice, and unto the voice of my servants whom I have appointed to lead my people, behold, verily I say unto you, they shall not be moved out of their place."

We must be able to recognize the voice of the Savior in our own hearts so that we will know if what we are doing is pleasing in his sight. When our leaders give us instructions, we can follow them with confidence because their voices harmonize with the voice of the Savior.

Sometimes well-meaning people do not even think about their own testimonies of the Savior. They have faith in their parents, they have faith in their spouses, they have faith in the bishop, they have faith in the manuals, and they have faith in the programs of the Church, but they have neglected to build their faith in Christ. All of those things are good things to have faith in under normal circumstances. All of them are worthy voices, loving voices, and righteous voices. But we all know, some through sorrowful experience, that not all fathers are worthy priesthood holders, that not all spouses are loving and self-sacrificing, that not all Church programs speak directly to our family's needs, and that not all manuals were written with us in mind. In such cases, is the answer to lose faith? No, it is to reassess our priorities and see if perhaps we are putting ultimate faith in people and places that are somewhat temporary. We need to build a stronger faith in the Savior. We need to hearken to his voice—to seek it, to listen carefully so that we can distinguish it from all others, and to pay attentive heed to its message.

If we feast on the scriptures, if we enter often into that limitless conversation with our Heavenly Father that we call prayer, and if we continually ask ourselves, "What would the Savior do or say if he were here now?" we are well on the way to having integrity of heart. When a decision needs to be made, we will know correct principles and we will not be swayed by the loudness of competing voices or by the popularity or authoritativeness of experts around us. We can make a decision that is right for us, even though it might not be right for someone else. We can help one child in a way that would be ineffective for a second child. We can choose what our priorities need to be for today, knowing that they will change tomorrow, and not feeling defensive because someone else's priorities are different.

That's what it means to have integrity of heart. Let me use Mother Teresa for an example. Once at a meeting in Bangalore, a sister criticized her for distributing food freely to the poor and said she was "spoiling" them. Mother Teresa answered: "If I spoil the poor, you and the other sisters spoil the rich in your select schools. And Almighty God is the first to spoil us. Does he not give freely to all of us? Then why should I not imitate my God and give freely to the poor what I have received freely?"[3]

I love that answer, not because it was a clever comeback, but because it referred the woman to a principle of the gospel in which they both believed. Mother Teresa was reminding her to listen to her own heart as she asked the question, "What would Jesus do?"

We live in fearsome times and need to meet those times with integrity of heart. We need, each one of us, to cultivate such a close relationship with the Savior that we can sort out his voice unerringly from among all of the other voices that clamor around us and can hear the messages that are personalized just for us, even among the good messages that come to all members of the Church. Then we can act with integrity.

It was on May 19, 1780—during the anxious days of our Revolutionary War—that darkness came at noon. The bats flew and chickens roosted. It was some sort of meteorological phenomenon that seemed to bring the day to an end when the sun was at zenith. Panic broke out, and people thought that the end of the world was at hand.

At Hartford, Connecticut, the State Legislature was in session and, when the darkness came at noon, the meeting of the Lower House broke up in alarm. In the State Senate a motion of adjournment was made, so that the legislators could meet the Day of Judgment with whatever courage they could manage to summon.

But the motion was opposed by Abraham Davenport, a Yankee selectman and judge, friend and advisor of George Washington. . . .

He arose and addressed his legislative colleagues. "I am against this adjournment," he said. Then he explained with a logic of courage: "The Day of Judgment," he said, "is either approaching or it is not. If it is not, there is no cause for adjournment. If it is, I choose to be found doing my duty. I wish, therefore, that candles may be brought."[4]

This is exactly the choice that faces us, day in and day out. We too can be found doing our duty, even in the darkest times. And the light and life of the world, the Savior and his love, will be a candle as we work.

7

SIMPLE HUMAN KINDNESS

When the apostle Paul says, "Charity suffereth long, and is kind" (1 Corinthians 13:4), he's not just talking about being nice and wearing smiley-face buttons. He's talking about the core of the disciple's life. Kindness without love is not kindness at all. It's patronage, it's condescension, it's smugness and superiority. If you have been the recipient of this species of "kindness," you know that you would much rather do without it. But with love, kindness is refreshment and rejoicing. It strengthens bonds and creates new ones. And it's a tough, patient virtue, not a frilly, fluffy one. It is significant to me that in the same verse in which Paul says charity is kind, he describes a second virtue, patience, in four different ways: charity "suffereth long, . . . is not easily provoked, . . . beareth all things, . . . endureth all things" (1 Corinthians 13:4–7). In other words, a charitable person must endure in patience, endure more than her share, suffer when it is not fair, and suffer "long." Kindness is not sentimental or weak. It's tough, strong, and long-lasting.

Mother Teresa has said:

> It is not very often *things* [the poor] need. What they need much more is what we offer them. In these twenty years of work amongst the people, I have come more and more to realize

that it is being unwanted that is the worst disease that any human being can ever experience. Nowadays we have found medicine for leprosy and lepers can be cured. There's medicine for TB and consumptives can be cured. For all kinds of diseases there are medicines and cures. But for being unwanted, except there are willing hands to serve and there's a loving heart to love, I don't think this terrible disease can ever be cured.[1]

I want to second Mother Teresa's motion. Simple human kindness is the cure and it has to come from within us, not from outside us. Kindness is not complicated. It's little things, done consistently, with a cumulative impact.

The Savior set the example of kindness for us. He healed the sick, made the lame walk, opened the eyes of the blind, and restored dead children to the arms of their mothers. He watches over all of us with tender care, unfailing hope, and boundless love. One of the loveliest promises of the scriptures is a view of the next world in which we will be allowed to bear our testimonies of the Savior:

> And now the year of my redeemed is come; and they shall mention the loving kindness of their Lord, and all that he has bestowed upon them according to his goodness, and according to his loving kindness, forever and ever.
>
> In all their afflictions he was afflicted. And the angel of his presence saved them; and in his love, and in his pity, he redeemed them, and bore them, and carried them all the days of old. (D&C 133:52–53)

Few motivations to serve the Savior are as strong as the motive of having felt his loving kindness in our own lives. We turn, almost as if by instinct, to reach out in kindness to others.

Sometimes we feel we don't have enough time or resources to make a difference in someone's life. It's all right to do what you can, no matter how small that is. In a collection of letters children wrote to God, I was very touched by one letter from a little girl who wrote: "Dear God, I am sending you a penny to give a kid poorer than me. Love. Donna."[2] A penny isn't much. To most of us it would be nothing, maybe not even worth stooping to pick up from the sidewalk. But what it showed was the kindness in this little girl's heart. There's nothing insignificant about that!

Let me give you another example of a small kindness. I remember reading a story about a man on a city bus who was confronted with a need. A woman in a front seat of the bus was slouched down, obviously weary and even dazed.

> Her hair was matted, her face dirty, and though it was a cold night outside, she was wearing only a flimsy cotton dress and a blanket through which she had torn holes for her arms.
>
> *What should I do?* I wondered. She was so obviously in need. And at Christmastime too. Wasn't there some shelter I could direct her to, some place where she'd get all the attention she required? No, I finally reasoned, her problems were too much for me.
>
> As I pondered—and rejected—possible solutions to the woman's plight, the bus came to a stop. A young man, poorly dressed but neat, rose to leave. He had got out and the bus had started up again before I really noticed what he had done. He had slipped off his black knit gloves and laid them on her lap.[3]

That young man could not solve the woman's problems and he did not try. Anyway, he was getting off the bus at the next stop. But he saw her cold, red hands and knew there was something he could do about them. And he did it.

At Holly Hills Elementary School where I was principal, Russ, our building engineer, came rushing into my office one afternoon with two yellow sheets of paper. Excitedly, he said, "See what these two little kindergarten girls gave me!" On the yellow sheets were crayon pictures of smiling children, pretty flowers, other objects requiring further interpretation by a kindergartner, and words written in print sliding downhill that said, "To Russ, I love you." They had made Russ a very happy man with something so simple.

Kindness is no more complicated than a yellow piece of construction paper with print sliding downhill. We can all say a simple thank you. None of those things I have mentioned took more than a few minutes. In fact, if we put everything together, I doubt that all of those interchanges would add up to even a half hour. We are in a position every day to do such kindnesses—at home, on the way to work, for the busy and burdened people with whom we work, for the friends and families and especially the strangers who telephone, hoping that the voice on the other end will be friendly and sympathetic. Kindness is like ripples in a pond, but instead of dying out as they spread out from the place where you throw in the rock, they just get stronger and the ties between us get more complex.

Somebody who is a real Saint, in my book, and a model for all of us in serving this way is Mary Cox. When I learned about her, she was eighty-three years old and a volunteer at the Utah County Youth Corrections, Observation, and Assessment Center for troubled teenagers. She tutored these kids in math; she also hugged them, listened to their problems, and told them they could make something of their lives. And they listened and called her "Grandma." She had been widowed early, left with three young children to support. In a farm accident, she had broken her back, and had worn a brace for thirty years. She'd also been a diabetic for twenty-seven years, had survived six major surgeries, and had used an oxygen tank twenty-four hours a day for the previous two years. Yet five days a week, she was at the center with her kids.

"I love them all," Mary said. "Each one is different. Some I get closer to than others, but I don't love one more than another. They have problems, but they are all good kids."

What would have happened if Grandma Mary had asked herself, "Do I really feel well enough to go tutor a bunch of teenagers in detention today?" I think she would have stayed home. Instead, the question she asked herself was, "Does somebody there need me?"[4]

Kindness is an addiction nobody would want to cure. Kindness multiplies and strengthens. It's like a chemical reaction—a good one—that doesn't stop, once it's set in motion.

A disciple's heart is kind spontaneously, because kindness is self-replenishing. Kindness establishes a confident, loving, generous relationship with another person, even if it's a stranger whom you will never see again. Consequently, kindness creates a confident, loving, generous *you*. You are not a victim, not an object of pity, when you are kind. I never cease to be astonished at how quickly and how satisfyingly the reward of feeling Christ's love comes with even a tiny act of kindness. It's a deeply powerful and empowering principle of the gospel. The Dalai Lama, when asked to describe the Tibetan religion, said, "My religion is very simple. My religion is kindness."[5] Isn't that a wonderful thought?

Having a kind heart can be a spiritual gift, but it can also be a skill that you learn. Our two sons, Ken and Bob, are seventeen months apart, so they were pretty closely matched in going through their developmental stages. Quite frequently, the same toy would look pretty good to both of them. We never allowed them to hit or fight or just grab, but we wanted them to be able to solve their own problems, too, so we didn't intervene unless it was necessary. Fortunately, we were also blessed with boys who had a strong sense of brotherly love for each other.

I remember one afternoon watching Ken as he tried to figure out how to persuade Bob to stop playing with the dump truck. Ken was about four and Bob was about three. Ken rummaged around in the toy box until he found a shiny red car. Then he drove it past Bob a couple of times, making tempting *vroom-vroom* noises. Bob looked up briefly, then went back to his own play.

"Look, Bob," Ken said persuasively, "did you know that this car can go like this?" He showed Bob how it could turn corners.

Fascinated, Bob reached for the car. "Sure, you can have it," said Ken. "Is it all right if I play with the truck?"

"Sure," Bob said. Two happy little boys, without a problem, settled down again to play—thanks to two things: Ken's kind heart and his competence at turning a potential conflict into a win/win situation.

I think maybe one of the reasons that our boys grew up to become gentle, kindly, Christlike men is because they had a wonderful example sitting across the kitchen table from them—their father. Whenever there was a problem, a difficulty at school, a decision that needed to be made, or a misunderstanding that needed to be rectified, Ed would always listen patiently and calmly, never showing any surprise or shock or dismay, no matter what the boys were saying. Then he would ask, "How do you feel about that?" And again, he would listen. (Sometimes the answers were lengthy and indignant!) And then, when the boys had had a chance to explain fully what they thought and felt, he would ask another question: "What would Jesus do?"

It got so that the boys could see it coming. Ed would just start to ask the question, and they'd finish it for him: "I know, I know! What would Jesus do?" Sometimes we'd all break up laughing about it. Sometimes they'd say it in a sarcastic voice. But nearly always the question led them to think about constructive solutions, approaches that they felt good about, ideas where they had the help of the Holy Ghost in thinking through the solution. And I think they came up with much better solutions than if they had asked questions like, "How can I get even?" or "How can I fix this so it won't happen again?"

There are many problems that can be solved with ordinary kindness. I read a book recently in which the author asked children how they would solve problems in the world. Some of the problems were global—like pollution or war—and some of the problems were the serious but more ordinary problems that occur just because of our human diversity. For example, she asked them: "How can you make people feel better about themselves?" Nine-year-old Katelyn suggested: "If they don't feel like they're pretty you could say, 'You're a lot prettier than a person I know who has big bulgy eyes.'"

And eight-year-old Jacqueline said: "Everyone should have an alarm clock that says nice things to them in the morning when they wake up." But I like the answer of eight-year-old Reem the best: "If someone says to me, 'I feel that no one likes me,' I would say, 'Well, I like you and if the people don't like you, they're not the right people for you. But the people that think you're special are special. Because deep inside your heart—*way* inside—if you really feel deep down, you'll find that you're special.'"[6]

Another point I want to make about kindness is that kindness has to come from within. We need to feel that kindness is its own reward. It's important to be kind for its own sake, not because there's going to be some great payoff (although the rewards of kindness are great) or because other people will notice how kind we are (although they likely will), or because we want to improve ourselves and our dispositions (although that will happen too). But we can't count on any external rewards.

One writer who has studied burnout in community volunteers comments on this weighty truth:

> If we're willing to help only perfect people, we might as well shut down everything right now because there aren't any perfect people out there to help.
>
> No, if you're going to survive volunteering, you can't do so because you think the people you're helping deserve it. You can't help people because they'll thank you. You have to help them because Christ loves them and He's loving them through you. You volunteer because in doing so, you represent Christ to them in the here and now—even if they don't see Him in you.[7]

We've all had some experience with kindness and unkindness, in our families, at school, with our friends, and in our classes. You know how it feels when someone is kind to you. And I hope you know the feeling in your own heart that happens when you're

81

kind to someone. It's a feeling that's hard to describe but easy to identify, and I think it has a great deal to do with the Spirit of the Lord. I want to testify from personal experience that nothing is more comforting during times of heartache than receiving the kindness of others—unless it's being able to perform a kindness.

I'm sure you've heard the saying, "If you want to feel better, do something for someone." Well, it's literally true. Take, for example, Laura Henrie, an eighty-eight-year-old woman living in Orem, Utah. She has arthritis and can't walk, but she can sit for hours, sewing doll clothes and baby outfits on her old Singer sewing machine, or crocheting and knitting.

> For Christmas [this year] she's been making lap afghans for residents of a nursing home.
>
> She said her granddaughter works as a dietician at a nursing home and she heard that so many of the residents there have few if any visitors and could maybe benefit from one of her handmade gifts.
>
> . . . Many years ago, when her own 15-year-old daughter Francis was killed in a traffic accident . . . , she worked out of the grief by helping others.
>
> "That Christmas, I made 70 little girl outfits and doll clothes to give away. And that was the most rewarding Christmas I had ever had. Instead of missing Franty, my heart went out to those I was helping," Laura said.
>
> She likes to say she could have felt "bitter" but says the second letter in bitter is "I." She said she chose to feel "better" where the second letter . . . is "E" for "everybody."[8]

Offer kindness where you can—even in the face of anger and rejection, even when fairness does not require it. One of the most touching stories I have ever heard was about an Austrian woman whose

> husband, a simple, uneducated Catholic farmer, decided he couldn't serve in Hitler's army because it would be an immoral

act. . . . Franziska, [his wife,] supported his decision even though they were desperately in love. Eventually, he was convicted of treason and condemned to death. The day before his execution, Franziska went to visit him for one last time in Brandenburg prison in Berlin. After watching him being cruelly hurled off a truck, hands and feet bound, she was led by two guards into a room with a long table and two chairs. [Her husband's hands and feet were untied, and he was led into the room; but] as she and her husband began to sit across from each other, one of the guards moved the chairs so that when they were sitting, they would be barely able to reach their hands across the table and touch. After an unimaginable last conversation, it was time to part. The other guard offered to bring the prisoner out, and the heartless guard left. The second guard then turned away from the couple long enough for them to rush into a last embrace. Waiting until their sobs quieted somewhat, he then said quietly, "It's time to go."[9]

That's perhaps a more dramatic setting than most of us will ever face, but there was nothing dramatic about the act of kindness itself. It was a small human decency that has remained vivid in memory for half a century. There was nothing this Nazi soldier could do about the husband's imprisonment or about the firing squad that was waiting, no way he could change the system he lived and worked in, and no way to protect the couple from the sadistic impulse of the first guard. But in the simple kindness of turning his back for a moment, he gave them one last meaningful moment together. You will have many opportunities to offer small kindnesses. Please, take every one you can.

Let me give you a personal example. In the fall of 1993, my husband's brother, Gordon, called from Hawaii to say that his wife had just been diagnosed as having pancreatic cancer. It was a terrible blow. Gordon and Viona had been so kind to me after Ed's death, and I had leaned on their strength. The doctors did not expect her to live very long—not past Christmas, but she surprised them all by retaining her strength in a remarkable manner. Christmas passed, a time of celebration and thanksgiving for her and her children. Viona had always been active in the Church, but Gordon was not a member, and they had never been sealed in the temple.

In early spring, Viona asked if I would speak at her funeral, and with her exquisite courtesy, she said to me, "I know that you are very busy, but if you could, I'd appreciate it." Then she added, "And if you will, would you tell all who come about the plan of salvation as we understand it?" I knew what she meant. She knew that members of the family would come to her funeral who hadn't set foot in the door of a church for most of their lives, and she wanted her funeral to be a time for them to hear the comforting news of the gospel of Jesus Christ.

This was a fearsome responsibility for me. My husband's death two years earlier was still fresh and painful in my mind. I knew this was going to be a hard thing for me to do, since Viona's death would bring up all of the feelings about Ed's death that I had tried to deal with patiently and faithfully. I was right. Many things about it were hard. But the kindest thing Viona did of the many kind things she did for me was to make me part of her dying, despite the distance that separated us.

I accompanied her to the temple where she was able to fulfill her lifelong dream of being endowed and making in her body the covenants that she had had a worthy heart for all of her life. Despite her great desire for an eternal marriage, she acted with great kindness toward Gordon, putting no pressure on him to make a decision for her sake or in the emotion of that stressful time that he might later feel was not his own. She respected his agency, even though their temple sealing was something she had longed for all of their married life.

What a privilege it was for me to select her temple clothing and help her put it on for the first time in the temple, knowing that it would also be her burial clothing. It was another example of

Viona's kindness to me—to let me do this for her as a way of showing some of the love I felt for her.

Before she died, Viona had asked forgiveness for any hard feelings she might have provoked with members of the family. Standing on the threshold of eternity, she reached back to help those who still have a few years to spend in mortality lift their eyes from a history of misunderstanding and grievance to see a bright picture of forgiveness and hope. In this, I see the action of a Christlike person—filled with love, pointing the way to a better life, and teaching all of us to do better.

But Viona's ultimate kindness to me was in asking me to speak at her funeral about the plan of salvation. In the presence of death, there is no room for falseness or insincerity or high-sounding platitudes devoid of real substance. I have believed in the plan of salvation ever since the missionaries first taught it to me when I was a teenager, and it was a great comfort to me during Ed's death. But the reality of it had never struck home in so forceful and profoundly reassuring a way as it did when I spoke at Viona's funeral about our choice to accept mortality, the joy with which we welcomed this experience, and the eternal love that awaits us in the world to come. I have never felt such gratitude for the Savior's atoning sacrifice or felt such a renewed desire to serve him and truly become his disciple. Real comfort came to me, real clarity enlightened my mind, and a renewed desire for righteousness was born in my own heart.

What this experience teaches me is that we are never beyond the power to do a kindness for someone else. Standing on the very point of death, Viona continued to act with the same spirit of kindness that had animated her whole life. If she can do it, we all can do it.

I was thrilled by President Howard W. Hunter's invitation to the members of the Church

> to live with ever more attention to the life and example of the
> Lord Jesus Christ, especially the love and hope and compassion

He displayed. I pray that we might treat each other with more kindness, more courtesy, more humility and patience and forgiveness. We do have high expectations of one another, and all can improve. Our world cries out for more disciplined living of the commandments of God. But the way we are to encourage that, as the Lord told the Prophet Joseph in the wintry depths of Liberty Jail, is "by persuasion, by long-suffering, by gentleness and meekness, and by love unfeigned; . . . without hypocrisy, and without guile" (D&C 121:41–42).[10]

This is an invitation to kindness that we can all accept. It is sobering to me to realize that President Hunter issued this invitation as he himself stood on the threshold of death. It is yet another reminder that we can afford to let no occasion pass to act on the disciple's value of kindness. Kindness has a boundless ability to fill us, brimming and overflowing, with a life that has meaning and significance.

The apostle Paul told the Corinthians how they could recognize a true representative of the Lord Jesus Christ. How? "By pureness, by knowledge, by longsuffering, by kindness, by the Holy Ghost, by love unfeigned" (2 Corinthians 6:6). May we who bear the name of Jesus Christ represent him well through our knowledge, our kindness, and the inborn knowledge that we are infinitely precious to him, in whatever place our lives and the Spirit take us.

8

RAISED IN HOPE

As disciples of the Lord Jesus Christ, we embrace the great trio of virtues: faith, hope, and charity. They help us lift and strengthen one another with love, testimony, faith, and service to each other. It is the second of these virtues, hope, that I wish to explore.

I think of hope as a modest but solid, everyday virtue, an ordinary but resilient virtue that is both gentle and beautiful. It is an unassuming but powerful force for good that will greatly increase our ability to do good and to be good.

Let me compare it to an ingenious fan-hat that was given to me in Tonga as a present from the Relief Societies when I was visiting the stakes there. If it's hot and muggy, you can use the fan to create a cooling breeze, and its curved ribs provide even a greater current of air than a flat fan. But if it should start to rain, the fan can quickly become a hat and provide shelter from the storm. In much the same way, hope is a virtue for all seasons and all adversities, whether the problem is a storm or too much pleasant weather.

What is the opposite of hope? Despair, of course, but despair comes when we feel powerless to influence events and when the sources of meaning in our life disappear. Despair is a kind of disorientation so profound that we lose contact with the sources of life itself.

I'm not a very good gardener, and I recently noticed that a carelessly placed brick had squashed a pansy flat. But part of the pansy was still peeking out from under the edge of the brick. Over the next few weeks, that pansy put its energies into creeping sideways around the edge of the brick, pushing its short shoots into the air and sunlight, and blossoming in its friendly purple and gold. When I moved the brick, the pansy's stem was crooked—but oh, its flower was as glorious as those next to it.

This pansy chose life. It experienced adversity, but it chose life. It experienced crippling, but it chose life. It could not have been blamed or faulted for giving up under the brick, but it chose life.

The sources of hope are the sources of life itself. That's why hope persists, even when experience, reason, and knowledge all say there is no reason to hope. Hope does not calculate odds. It is a double-sided virtue. Like the fan-hat, it is prepared for either sunny or stormy weather. To choose hope is to choose life. To choose hope is to choose love.

The Lord told the ancient Israelites, after giving them the laws and commandments of Deuteronomy:

> I call heaven and earth to record this day against you, that I have set before you life and death, blessing and cursing: therefore *choose life*, that both thou and thy seed may live:
>
> That thou mayest love the Lord thy God, and that thou mayest obey his voice, and that thou mayest cleave unto him: for he is thy life, and the length of thy days. (Deuteronomy 30:19–20; emphasis added)

Why is this so? Why is hope so intimately tangled with the roots of life itself? Hope is one of the three great Christian virtues because Christ himself is the master of life and therefore the master of hope. We are free to choose because we were made free from the beginning, and he honors our agency and our right and ability to choose. The choice he offers is life, and life offers hope. Any other choice is a choice of spiritual death that will bring us into the power of the devil.

And now, I hope it is clearer why part of that hope in Christ is hope in the future, a future that includes resurrection and salvation and exaltation. Paul explained to the Romans that Christ submitted himself to death but, "being raised from the dead dieth no more; death hath no more dominion over him" (Romans 6:9). Jesus Christ, our Savior, has always been the master of life, but through his atoning sacrifice, he also became the master over death. Physical death has no dominion over him, and ultimately it has no dominion over us because of Christ.

Think what this means! Because of our Savior's victory, we too can be victorious. In the face of this good news, this triumph shout from the battlefield of ultimate victory, we can see why our everyday sacrifices, our ordinary hope is so tough, so versatile, so difficult to turn into meaninglessness and despair.

In fact, it cannot happen—we literally cannot despair—unless we choose to. But because we are mortal, death is entangled with life. We can choose to feed the darkness and death in our lives, or we can choose to feed the brightness of hope in our lives. We can worry. We can deny the light. We can refuse to ally ourselves with Jesus Christ, the already triumphant master of life. We can give our lives piece by piece into captivity until we no longer have the power to wrench it away again. We can cooperate with the killing of our spirits and the strangling of our hopes until meaninglessness and despair overcome us. The death of the body is nothing—for Christ's resurrection guarantees our own—but he cannot rescue us from the death of the spirit unless we choose to ally ourselves with him, with his hope, with the inexhaustible and irrepressible life that is his.

But I testify that the forces of life are *always* stronger than the forces of death. If we choose, if we even desire to choose, if we even hope for the desire to choose, we set in motion powerful forces for life that are led by Jesus Christ himself. He responds to those tender tendrils of crippled life with the force and energy that will bring them to flowering. Listen to these promises of love and yearning desire for us. Feel the hope they bring that with him we can overcome the world.

"I am the door," he said. "By me if any [one] enter in, he shall be saved." In contrast to the thief of life, which he says is come only to "steal, and to kill, and to destroy," Jesus "[is] come that [we] might have life, and that [we] might have it more abundantly. I am the good shepherd," he assures us. "The good shepherd giveth his life for the sheep" (John 10:9–11).

The Psalmist sang:

> Whither shall I go from thy spirit? or whither shall I flee from thy presence?
>
> If I ascend up into heaven, thou art there: if I make my bed in hell, behold, thou art there.
>
> If I take the wings of the morning, and dwell in the uttermost parts of the sea;
>
> Even there shall thy hand lead me, and thy right hand shall hold me. (Psalm 139:7–10)

And in our own day, Jesus Christ spoke through Joseph Smith: "And as I said unto mine apostles, even so I say unto you, . . . ye are they whom my Father hath given me; ye are my friends" (D&C 84: 63). "And [ye] shall be mine in that day when I shall come to make up my jewels" (D&C 101:3).

O dear friend, choose life, even though the forces of death seem strong! Choose hope, even though despair seems close. Choose to grow, even though circumstances oppress you. Choose to learn, even though you must struggle against your own ignorance and that of others. Choose to love, even though ours are days of violence and vengeance. Choose to forgive, to pray, to bless another's life with simple kindness, to strengthen another with love, testimony, faith, and service. I promise that you will feel the abundant love of the Savior. He receives each act of mercy to one of the least as one done to himself. And in return he defies hopelessness, weariness, despair, and meaninglessness on our behalf.

The apostle Paul asked, "Who shall separate us from the love of Christ? shall tribulation, or distress, or persecution, or famine, or nakedness, or peril, or sword?" Then came his magnificent answer:

> Nay, in all these things we are more than conquerors through him that loved us.
>
> For I am persuaded, that neither death, nor life, nor angels, nor principalities, nor powers, nor things present, nor things to come,
>
> Nor height, nor depth, nor any other creature, shall be able to separate us from the love of God, which is in Christ Jesus our Lord. (Romans 8:35–39)

I testify that my Christ is my hope. He is my hope on rainy Monday mornings, my hope on dark nights, and my hope in the face of death and despair. And I bear this living testimony in his holy name, even the name of my Lord and Savior Jesus Christ.

9

WHO WE ARE, WHOSE WE ARE

Do you ever have times when you're not quite sure who you are? I read a funny story about Elder Bruce R. McConkie and a sort of identity crisis that he had one weekend. In 1971, Elder McConkie wrote a letter to Elder Marion D. Hanks after he got back from a stake conference in Torrance, California, where he had been mistaken for several other people. He wrote:

> The Stake President introduced me by saying how grateful they were to have Brother *Hinckley* with them and to partake of his wonderful spirit and superior counsel. [A brother] who was sitting by me on the stand looked askance. I acted as though nothing was amiss, figuring if I pretended to be Brother Hinckley, perhaps things would go better than otherwise. . . . After the meeting, a devout sister . . . grasped my hands . . . and said, "Oh, Brother *Packer;* that was the greatest sermon I have ever heard in all my experience in the Church." . . .
>
> Today as I walked up 2nd East, an oversized limousine . . . pulled up to the curb and [the driver] called out, "Oh, Brother *Hanks,* if I don't give this to you to give to your wife, my wife will kill me when I get home." I thanked him, took the package and said, "I'll be happy to deliver it to my wife." After more

mature reflection, I think I might perhaps impose upon you to
deliver it to Maxine [Elder Hanks's wife].

Sincerely,

Your brother of questionable identity

A. Theodore McConkie

P.S. I am taking the liberty of sending a copy of this memo to
Boyd Monson, so that he will be apprised of what a great sermon
he preached.[1]

I want to tell you another story about "questionable identities." When my younger grandson, Andrew, was just two and a
half, his parents were busy preparing for a move from Wisconsin
to Colorado, where Bob was starting a new job. They were buying
a new house. There was all the work of packing in the old house
and making arrangements to move into the new house. And there
was Halloween, too. Bob's wife, Chris, had saved a mouse costume that Matthew, Andrew's older brother, had worn when he
was Andrew's age; she thought, "At least I'll have to worry about
only one costume!" Well, she was wrong. Matthew was going to
be a jet pilot, and to his adoring little brother, Andrew, being a jet
pilot was just about the most exciting thing he could think of. So
when the topic of the mouse came up, he was not very excited. I
called about ten days before Halloween and talked to Andrew.

"What are you going to be for Halloween, Andrew?" I asked.

"Me jet!" he announced firmly.

"Oh," I said. "You want to be a jet like Matthew? But what
about the mouse costume? Who will be the mouse?"

There was a long silence on the line. I could tell that this was a
big problem for Andrew. But he found a way to solve it. The next
time I called, just a few days later, he announced triumphantly,
"Me jet, Nana. Dad mouse!"

Well, there were a few unsolved problems with that particular
scenario. Perhaps the most important one was that Bob is about six
feet tall. But the point I want to make is that Andrew, just age two
and a half, somehow felt responsible for his mouse identity and

didn't feel completely free to be a jet until he had found someone to take his place as a mouse. Chris, bless her heart, was able to find a cape and a pilot's helmet and a few other things so Andrew could fly around as happy as a lark. There's a lot about agency and love in this little family experience.

Sometimes we have identities assigned to us. Someone has a mouse costume for us to wear when what we want to be is a jet. This happens a lot in families. And a lot of these costumes, or identities, really are good things to put on—things like the good student costume, or the responsible helper costume, or the organizer costume, or the communicator costume. You may have even done some experimenting with identities. I'm not going to talk about negative identities. You know what they are, and you know how a wrong choice makes you feel when you have to live with it.

Instead, let's talk about the range of identities that are all good, and all available to us because we are free to choose. What about the identity of being interested in others, of being caught up in a social cause, of being available for service projects, of taking a class in art when you don't know which end of a paintbrush to hold? These experiments are good. They push back your boundaries. They broaden your horizons. They increase your skills.

Wise parents and wise teachers can challenge children's identities in ways that will stretch the limits of how they see themselves. Sherri and Ronald Zirker of Mesa, Arizona, tell of the time when their oldest son broke his right arm in such a way that he had to have a cast from his wrist up over his elbow. But after taking over his duties for a few days, his father told him that it was time for him to start milking the cow again. "Me?" he exclaimed. "I'm crippled!" Is that an identity? You bet it is! It's an identity that says, "I'm helpless. You need to do things for me."

Well, he had a father who was an expert at challenging identity in healthy ways. Ron assured the boy that he could do it, said he himself had milked cows with a broken arm, and sent his son out to the cow. To the family, he said, "Give him some time, show your confidence in his ability, and let him know you need him and depend on him to do it."

So they did. At first, this boy made only a half-hearted attempt, angling for sympathy; but when nobody rescued him or lectured him, and when the family went without milk, he buckled down to work. Within a week, the bucket was full again. Furthermore, he learned to write easily with his left hand; and during the month his arm was in the cast, he earned six merit badges at Scout camp. Do you think he'll sell his abilities short when he encounters obstacles later in his life? I think he'll have unusual self-confidence instead.

As important as knowing who we are is knowing *whose* we are. As King Benjamin reminded his people, "Because of the covenant which ye have made ye shall be called the children of Christ, his sons, and his daughters; for behold, this day he hath spiritually begotten you; for ye say that your hearts are changed through faith on his name; therefore, ye are born of him and have become his sons and his daughters" (Mosiah 5:7).

Think what it means to be a son or daughter of Christ. This is not just a pretty family metaphor. Our baptismal covenant enables us to enter into a new relationship with the Savior, to have new claims on his mercy, and to experience his grace and love in new ways. Because you are an individual, unique in the universe, irreplaceable, and inexpressibly precious to our Heavenly Father, you can never be blotted out or erased by the actions that anyone else does to you. You can never be made to feel like nothing or to become a nobody without your cooperation and consent. You can do it to yourself, but no one can do it to you.

I hope you know that even during the hardest moments of your life, when your powerlessness seems absolute and your isolation total, you are not alone. The Savior is with you, being with you as you endure the pain so that you can go on, healed and renewed. Your survival and even your triumph are assured through his atoning sacrifice and his love. Do you know that if you were the only person in the world who needed his atonement, he would still have died for you—just for you?

Whatever our circumstances, let us remember when the lost and lonely times come that there is no place where the love of the Savior does not find us and encircle us. We have the right to his love and his presence.

Think about whose you are, whose name you bear. I have always enjoyed the passage in Revelation 2:17 in which the angel tells John the Beloved, "To him that overcometh will I give to eat of the hidden manna, and will give him a white stone, and in the stone a new name written, which no man knoweth saving he that receiveth it." And of course this passage would apply to women as well. The Prophet Joseph Smith referred directly to this passage and then explained:

> Then the white stone mentioned in Revelation 2:17, will become a Urim and Thummim to each individual who receives one, whereby things pertaining to a higher order of kingdoms will be made known;
>
> And a white stone is given to each of those who come into the celestial kingdom, whereon is a new name written, which no man knoweth save he that receiveth it. The new name is the key word. (D&C 130:10–11)

We're not in the celestial kingdom yet, and I don't know whether the white stone is literal or figurative, but I think that this is the Lord's way of reminding us about the importance of the names we choose to take upon us—to choose names of honor and valor, names that we can bear proudly and pass on unsullied to our children. What do you think when you hear the name "Adolf Hitler"? Is that a name you want for your own? No! What about your family name? What about your personal name or names? And what about the name of Christ that you bear as a result of having been baptized and having accepted that name by covenant?

The Lord promised the Israelites through Isaiah: "For as the new heavens and the new earth, which I will make, shall remain before me, saith the Lord, so shall your seed and *your name* remain (Isaiah 66:22; emphasis added). In Jeremiah, we read another of the Lord's promises: "Behold, the days come, . . . that I will make a new covenant with the house of Israel" (Jeremiah 31:31). Ezekiel summoned his people to a new effort with this challenging scripture: "Cast away from you all your transgressions, whereby ye have transgressed; and make you a new heart and a new spirit" (Ezekiel 18:31). What is the gospel about if it is not about renewal? about putting off the old and putting on the new? about growing so that we match our eternal potential instead of being satisfied with our earthly limitations? As the apostle Paul explained, "Therefore if any man [or woman] be in Christ, he [or she] is a new creature: old things are passed away; behold, all things are become new" (2 Corinthians 5:17).

Isn't this what the Lord promises us when he holds out before us the joy of repenting, the hope of new covenants with him, and the rejoicing of being a new creature in Christ? We're not dolls that passively submit to being washed and restitched and clothed. We're living, loving creatures in our own right who can make and keep covenants, choose the right, endure to the end, and rejoice, as Joseph Smith promised the Saints of his day, "that we may ever be with the Lord, That our garments may be pure, that we may be clothed upon with robes of righteousness, with palms in our hands, and crowns of glory upon our heads, and reap eternal joy for all our sufferings" (D&C 109:75–76).

You are a beloved son or daughter of our Heavenly Parents. Their hearts yearn over you in joy and love. They want to give you all the treasures of eternity, and they hope steadfastly that you will be the kind of person who will want the riches of eternity— in other words, that you will follow the pathway marked out for you by the Savior and live a life that is guided by the principle of love. Remember little Andrew, exercising his agency to choose between the two good options of being a mouse or being a jet, and remember Chris, at a busy time in her life, finding that extra ounce of love to honor a little boy's agency because she loved him. Remember the boy learning how to milk a cow with his arm in a cast—rejecting the identity of the "cripple" (mostly because his dad wouldn't take no for an answer) and accepting the identity of someone who didn't let handicaps stop him. Remember that who you are is only the beginning of who you can be.

And remember *whose* you are. You are the Savior's. As the apostle Paul explained to the Corinthians:

> Know ye not that your body is the temple of the Holy Ghost which is in you, which ye have of God, and ye are not your own?
>
> For ye are bought with a price: therefore glorify God in your body, and in your spirit, which are God's. (1 Corinthians 6:19–20)

Our Savior paid the price in the Garden of Gethsemane to snatch your soul from the bonds of death and hell and release you into his glorious light, to be free forever if you will choose the way of life and love and avoid the path of sin and death.

Let me close with the comforting words of the apostle Paul, reminding the Saints that a day would come when they would have a perfect knowledge of who they were and whose they were.

> For now we see through a glass, darkly; but then face to face: now I know in part; but then shall I know even as also I am known.
>
> And now abideth faith, hope, charity, these three; but the greatest of these is charity. (1 Corinthians 13:12–13)

May we rejoice in the perfect charity of the Savior, the Son of God, who became a helpless baby in a manger that he might experience mortality with us, bear our burdens with us, grieve with us, and rejoice with us.

10

LIFELONG LEARNING AND LITERACY

Nearly a billion people on the earth today are illiterate, and almost two-thirds of them are women. U.S. government studies suggest that as many as 20 percent of adults may be functionally illiterate—unable to fill out job applications or understand instructions on a bottle of medicine.[1] Sometimes it's easy to dismiss people who are functionally illiterate as being stupid or lazy. They are neither. They have learned how to read us. They've found ways to hide their own lack of literacy. They can cope. They can adjust. We need to be equally literate about each other's feelings and capacity to understand.

Anyone who is a lifelong learner seeks out and thrives in educational settings, and the setting itself provides not only knowledge but the tools to continue to acquire knowledge. Your literacy can and will take many forms, but all of them can be ways of helping others—men, women, and children.

The Relief Society has been engaged in an ongoing effort to encourage literacy. In an affluent, highly educated area, literacy projects have included creating reading lists with grandchildren and volunteering in the schools. In other areas, adults have fallen through the cracks of the American educational system or are learning English as a second language. And abroad, there are numerous areas where an education is simply not one of the privileges that people can afford. In such areas, women are using the literacy program developed, in part, by Brigham Young University professors for use in developing nations to begin at the beginning with the alphabet and teach reading, writing, and simple math computation.

Many things are happening as Relief Societies all over the world implement the literacy effort. But rather than focusing on how the program operates or how to make it work in your area, I'd like to discuss the principles underlying literacy—principles of lifelong learning, growth and strength, and unfailing pleasure for us all. For learning is delightful; we are all hungry to learn; our minds are designed to learn. We all need to become literate in many things. Learning is an activity that can bring us together in service and increase our love for God and for each other.

The Joy of Learning

Marva Collins, a respected black educator and founder of Westside Preparatory School in Chicago, says: "When someone is taught the joy of learning, it becomes a life-long process that never stops, a process that creates a logical individual. That is the challenge and joy of teaching."[2]

We are born to learn. We came here to earth to learn. We are hungry for knowledge, starving for understanding. Consequently, we are learning all the time. And the Lord likes that! Remember what he told the Prophet Joseph Smith?

> Teach ye diligently and my grace shall attend you, that you may be instructed more perfectly in theory, in principle, in doctrine, in the law of the gospel, in all things that pertain unto the kingdom of God, that are expedient for you to understand;
>
> Of things both in heaven and in the earth, and under the earth; things which have been, things which are, things which must shortly come to pass; things which are at home, things

which are abroad; the wars and the perplexities of the nations, and the judgments which are on the land; and a knowledge also of countries and of kingdoms. (D&C 88:78–79)

We can take all knowledge for our scope. We can learn many things and they will be delightful and profitable to us and to others. I know that many people today feel that learning needs to be circumscribed and carefully prescribed and supervised, that knowledge is dangerous. I agree that it can be. I am sickened by the sources of hate, of pornography, and of violence in our society. But I have a very simple test: Will what I am learning increase the amount of love in the world? Will it increase my love for others and my love for the Savior?

If the answer is yes, then that source of learning is good, no matter where it comes from. And often, the answer is more neutral—it will not *decrease* my love for the Savior or for others. Under those circumstances, I place very few restrictions on learning. And I think everyone should be very free to explore widely, to ask interesting and challenging questions, and to make sense of difficult topics. The best way to do that is in a supportive and rich environment where ideas can bump up against each other and where we can ask questions without fear of being rebuked. We do not learn by excluding information and announcing that we have the one true way to clean our house, to understand American history, to plant radishes in the spring, or to make democracy work.

Let me give you an example of how versatile we human beings are as learners. I've been a schoolteacher for twenty-three years and a principal for another ten. In those thirty-three years, I've seen literally dozens of reading programs come and go. They come because somebody gets a good idea, and the idea works because children have discovered the magic of reading on their own. Lately there's been a lot of attention on teaching early reading to preschoolers. Many parents have consulted me to find out what the best program is. And do you know what? Any program will work. They're all effective. Children will learn to read as long as they have letters, books, and teachers and parents who think reading is important. Of course it takes work, but all kinds of work pay off.

Learning is inherently satisfying. Reading is inherently rewarding. When reading is part of a loving relationship with a parent, learning to read by any method will work. We discover many ways to teach literacy when we consider it to be a principle of awareness, a way to enter into a relationship, and a way of having personal power in a given situation. For instance, I recall a second-grader whom I'll call Gary. He was having a difficult time learning to read, and the conventional methods that worked with the other children seemed to leave him frustrated and frightened. I could have insisted that he learn in the same way. I could have threatened, scolded, encouraged, and hammered away until he was able to mumble his way through a sentence, but then reading would have become the battleground for a negative relationship between the two of us. I wanted him to connect primarily with the power and joy of reading, not with an adult who was dissatisfied with him.

Gary was a good artist, so I let him draw a lot. Then I decided I could teach him to read through his drawings. He would tell me stories about the drawings, and I would write them down as he dictated them. Then I would put the story strip under the picture and ask, "Which word says *sky?* Which word says *car?* Which word says *fun?*" This was not a threatening or frightening system for Gary. These were his own words, his own picture, his own power. He learned to read easily and quickly after that.

My grandson Matthew was introduced to books early in his life. Naturally I think he's a bright little boy who was very responsive to learning, but he also had an extraordinarily rich learning environment at home. His parents always sat down daily with him and read with him, pointing out the words. The Christmas that he was four, my husband and I were going out to spend a few days with them and called them before we came. Matthew said, "Bring me books, Nana. And not those little short books! I want big books." His mother told me that they were reading the Boxcar Children series—meaning that his parents were reading the books to him and he was sounding out some of the simple words in them.

I said to him, "Oh, Matthew! That's really great. But these books have no pictures in them."

"That's right, Nana," he said. "I have to use my remagination."

Matthew was learning more than just the skill we ordinarily think of as literacy. He was learning something about his own power to learn and also something about his ability to interact as an active learner. The idea is that he's comfortable. He associates reading with good things.

I hope I've convinced you that we are all lifelong learners—that learning almost anything will bring us pleasure and satisfaction and joy because that's how we're designed as human beings. I think of Adam and Eve after they had been cast out of the garden, praying earnestly and faithfully offering sacrifice until an angel of the Lord appeared to them and explained the plan of salvation. Do you remember what happened next? They rejoiced because of what they had learned:

> And in that day Adam blessed God and was filled, and began to prophesy concerning all the families of the earth, saying: Blessed be the name of God, for because of my transgression my eyes are opened, and in this life I shall have joy, and again in the flesh I shall see God.
>
> And Eve, his wife, heard all these things and was glad, saying: Were it not for our transgression we never should have had seed, and never should have known good and evil, and the joy of our redemption, and the eternal life which God giveth unto all the obedient.
>
> And Adam and Eve blessed the name of God, and they made all things known unto their sons and their daughters. (Moses 5:10–12)

They are describing the learning of gospel truths, but I know from my own experience that all learning brings joy to us. Learning the things of God and the things of eternity brings joy of a special and lasting kind, because our deepest hunger is to understand the things of God and to learn to be like him. But any learning will call into being a reflection—even if it's just a flicker—of the joy of Adam and Eve who blessed God for what they had learned.

Cultural Literacy

Not all learning is formal classroom learning. We all need to learn many, many things. I want to discuss next what some people call cultural literacy.

Let me demonstrate with a little cultural literacy quiz. 1492: Why is this date important? And June 8, 1978? If you know the answers to both questions, you have demonstrated your literacy in both American and Mormon history. But is it possible that in a different culture you might be perceived as illiterate? "In many traditional black societies, for example," writes Val Johnson, "musical ability is more highly esteemed than intellectual prowess. Indeed, in two languages the word *stupid* would be literally translated as 'one who cannot sing.'" What would "literacy" consist of in those cultures? It makes you stop and think, doesn't it?

Brother Johnson reports on the conscious efforts to identify and build a gospel culture that transcends and unites the many cultures of South Africa. Johann Brummer, an educator living in Johannesburg, asks an interesting question: "What is the essence of the gospel—that unchangeable and unchanging center which you cannot adapt to other cultures? Which aspects of a particular culture, for example, are healthy and wholesome parts of a people's identity and needn't be changed—and which aspects are peripheral, things they would be better off without?"

One member of the Church described how the transformation

of conversion created the ability to transcend cultural barriers. He said, "Since joining the Church, I forget there are other nationalities. Whenever I look at somebody now, I see a brother. The only thing I wish is to tell these people what joy is inside me."

Christoffel Golden, president of the Pretoria Stake, said: "The gospel brings a spirit into people's lives which heals and also covers many of the so-called differences we have. I've also learned that before the Lord, all people are equal, yet all people are diverse.

"And I don't think there's a weakness in diversity," he continued. "I think there's a strength. As the Church continues to grow, members worldwide will learn what we have learned here in South Africa—that the inclusion of more and more cultures will dramatically enrich the Church and give it greater strength than it has ever had before."[3]

My point is really simple. We have much to learn, and we can learn from almost anyone as long as we don't create barriers by thinking that what we have is more important than what they have, or by assuming that some people can't teach us anything.

Being culturally literate requires a certain amount of humility. If we think we already know everything, or at least all the important things, we don't bother to listen and we don't try to learn. And how can we help people if we communicate arrogance and contempt for their own system? I think of the old story about the smart young graduate from the agricultural college who came bustling out, full of knowledge, to the weather-beaten farmer who had barely passed eighth grade. The young man was sure he had the solution to all the farmer's problems, and he talked on and on while the farmer listened, polite but obviously unimpressed. Trying to make his point, the young graduate gestured at the animals grazing in the pasture and said challengingly, "Why, Farmer Jones, if you were to try my methods, I'll bet you'd get ten gallons of milk apiece from those cows."

The farmer perked up. "Well, son," he said, "if you could do that, I'd be *real* interested in your methods. Them's horses."

I learned a little humility about literacy myself once when I was taking care of my two grandsons while their parents were away. At age six, Matthew was practically grown up, but two-year-old Andrew sometimes struggled to communicate across the barriers of his age, his lack of verbal facility, and my own inexperience with his names for things.

One morning while Matthew was still asleep, Andrew woke up and came out in the living room quite fretfully. "Measure, Nana," he said unhappily. "Me want measure." Well, I'd learned Andrew's names for quite a few things but that was a new one on me.

"Shoe, Andrew?" I asked, holding up his shoe.

"No, Nana," he wailed. "Measure."

"Mommy?"

No. Did he want to go to the bathroom? No. Maybe some juice? He accepted it, said, "Thank you," took one swig, and said, "No! Want measure!" Well, I was racking my brain trying to think of every word or combination of words that might possibly sound like "measure," and Andrew was getting more and more upset.

Finally, I was so desperate I even thought about waking up Matthew and asking him to translate for me. But I didn't want to do that. Wouldn't it be wonderful if there were some dictionary in Andrew-language so that I could meet his needs? But there wasn't. He cried for three or four minutes, but when I distracted him with a toy and then cooked breakfast for him, he forgot all about it. When Chris and Bob got home, I told them this story and then asked Chris, "What does he mean by 'measure'?" Surely his mom would know. Chris look baffled. "I haven't any idea," she admitted.

So the wonderful thing about literacy is that there is always more to learn, always something that even an expert hasn't learned yet.

Think about body language. A tapping foot shows impatience. A nod of the head speaks of agreement. A hand on the shoulder may mean, "I'm listening. I'm your friend. Go ahead. Speak freely."

But if the hand is too heavy, it may communicate, "You'd better have a good reason for what you did, or you'll catch it from me!"

Body language varies with culture. We've already talked about some African examples. In Navajo culture it's impolite to look another in the eyes while talking, yet to the Anglo, to look away is to communicate shiftiness, inattentiveness, or lack of respect. Think of the misunderstandings and bad experiences that would exist between those two cultures unless they learned to read each other. In southern European cultures, people stand face to face and close while they talk, perhaps only thirty centimeters apart. In northern Europe, conversationalists demand more like a meter's difference or they feel uncomfortable, invaded.

I think most of us notice culture only when we ourselves feel like outsiders. If you want a quick lesson in how your own culture is invisible to you, ask someone who has recently come back to activity in the Church what things or processes or language or behavior made him or her feel like an outsider for the first few times. Ask an immigrant about American culture. Ask a new mother about the culture of experienced mothers. Ask a divorced woman about the couple culture in the Church. Ask a freshman at college about academic culture. As I thought about this, it became clear to me why the Lord commanded the Israelites: "Love ye therefore the stranger: for ye were strangers in the land of Egypt" (Deuteronomy 10:19).

Women have many opportunities to teach cultural literacy—in the broad sense—to others, and not just in schools and in jobs, although those are certainly important places. Do we think of our homes as places for teaching literacy—and not just reading? Do you have a mother who needs to learn to fill out her own income tax forms or who needs to learn some consumer advocacy skills in dealing with her doctor? Could you help her do that? Is there an immigrant woman on your block who needs someone to take her shopping and show her how an American supermarket works? I think we're all conscious of how many things we have yet to learn, but I want to remind you that if you can drive a car, read a newspaper, operate ordinary appliances, balance a checkbook, or run a sewing machine, you have skills that someone close to you may lack.

Think about your friends, your ward members, your neighbors. Statistics suggest that someone you know is being abused—physically, emotionally, or sexually. You know a teenager who is pregnant out of wedlock or is at high risk for pregnancy. You know someone who is depressed, perhaps even suicidal. You know boys and men who can think of only violent solutions to problems, who need to learn the skills of communication and negotiation. You know someone who is a victim of domestic violence. You know someone else who is a victim of the more subtle but equally damaging messages that who she is isn't enough, what she knows doesn't count, and what she needs is less important than what someone else needs. Can you be sensitive and respectful in teaching children, young people, and adults how to stand up for themselves and learn to function competently in our society?

I have great admiration and respect for a black Relief Society president, Gladys Newkirk of Capitol Hill Ward, Suitland Stake. It's an inner-city ward near Washington, D.C. She explained that welfare problems were both a great challenge and a great opportunity in her area. For example, one woman asked the bishop to pay her rent, insurance, and food expenses. Gladys went over to conduct the usual interview and discovered that there was enough money coming into the household to provide for their needs "with some left over," but the money simply wasn't being managed wisely. The woman was making monthly payments on a telephone system so huge and complicated that Gladys thought it was a switchboard. Rather than getting angry or assuming that this woman was trying to rip off the Church, Gladys said, "Let's get a piece of paper and pen and go over your bills and make a budget." Compassionately, she added, "We have so many people coming off [government] assistance and they just didn't know. Nobody bothered to say, 'Let's try to get you to help yourself instead of making you dependent upon the Church.'"

One brother who wanted welfare had a limp, but Gladys said, "I know a lot of handicapped people who are working. You're dwelling on the things you can't do. Let's talk about the things that you can do. You drive a car all the time. Have you considered pizza delivery or a gas station where you can sit down?" He made all kinds of excuses, but Gladys just kept encouraging him to find a job that could accommodate his handicap. Almost a full year later, he called Gladys up very happily to say: "I call you and your husband so often when I need something. I just wanted to call and let you know that I'm okay. I'm delivering pizza. I feel good about myself, and the exercise I get from delivering pizzas is really good for me." Gladys added: "Sometimes we feel a little embarrassed that we're telling grown people how to spend their money, but that's help they need." Bless Gladys's heart. Her own need not to feel embarrassed does not drown her sense of compassion and realism and common sense. She's willing to give these people the help that they need to become competent in our culture and society. What a great teacher she is!

A variation of cultural literacy might be termed situational literacy. Some people are savvy about Wall Street. Others are street wise. Some know their way around the city bus system. Others are comfortable in a classroom. Don't you think one of the reasons gang membership appeals to young people is that they admire the sheer competence, however misapplied and misleading, of those who claim to be gang leaders? Sometimes we make one system much more important than others and give certain types of literacy a privilege that we deny to others. The well-educated Relief Society sister who has the opportunity of being a literacy tutor has a wonderful opportunity to learn from a welfare mother she is tutoring, but only if she doesn't unconsciously assume, "You're a welfare mother. You can't teach me anything." That welfare mother may have a great deal to teach this sister about situational literacy.

Let me give you a personal example of situational literacy. My mother must have known from the time I was a little child that I would one day leave her, leave the island, and leave our traditional culture, so she taught me principles—not just practices. Much of what she said was transmitting our traditional culture, of course. This is what any parent does who is trying to teach a child a reality map. She would tell me, for instance, not to swim when a storm had brought the Portuguese man-of-war, with its poisonous sting, near the beach. This is very useful information, but it is limited. It becomes irrelevant, for instance, in Utah.

But she also gave me important information that would let me construct my own map of reality. I was astonished, when I left home at age fourteen to become a maid and cook to earn my way through high school, that her teachings would come back to me and be an important and empowering guide. Even now, fifty years later, I remember that she told me, "When you are visiting in people's homes, look around and see what needs there are. See how you can meet those needs."

She was teaching me an attitude and a skill by teaching me that principle. She was teaching me situational literacy. As a result, I learned to observe my environment, to appraise a situation quickly, to read the attitudes and moods of those present, and to enter into a relationship with that situation—a relationship of service. This was a powerful tool for me. I see many people who are unobservant and passive. They do not see problems developing until they become huge, and then they don't know how to handle them because they have no active relationship with the situation. These individuals lack power because they lack skill; they lack an approach. Change frightens them, and they cope badly with it, often becoming victims or victimizers. How grateful I am for my mother's wise and powerful teaching.

Service

Another principle of literacy I want to mention is service. Being literate in your heart is a special gift, especially when, in order to give people the kind of help they really need, you must overcome their resistance to receiving it.

Jana Seiter, a sister missionary in Guatemala, wrote us a beautiful letter about her involvement in the literacy program. She and her companion were teaching in Tiquisate, Guatemala, and contacted José, a man lying in a hammock. José was baptized two weeks later and now joyously stands at the door of the chapel greeting people before meetings. His next-door neighbor, Rosa, rented a single room where she lived alone. The sisters tried to teach her, but she was very defensive about the new truths of the gospel. So instead, the sisters offered to teach José and Rosa to read, using the orange literacy manuals where students begin with simple words like *God* and *love*. Sister Seiter writes:

> After José's baptism we offered to teach him and Rosa to read. Almost every Wednesday and Sunday afternoon they sit waiting for us outside their rooms with their orange manuals in hand. Rosa wears thick, black-rimmed glasses that are held together with a piece of yarn and elastic strip that she slips around her head. Sometimes I feel like they are the real teachers, especially when Rosa carefully lays out clothes before Hermana Kniskern sits down on the hot cement slab and when José insists that I sit in his prized wooden chair. I teach José; Hermana Kniskern teaches Rosa. I wish you could hear them pray when they ask God to please help them to learn to read his holy word. They also pray for us, thanking God for our health, our safety, our testimonies, our love, and asking Him to continue blessing us in our missionary work.
>
> . . . Somewhere between Joseph Smith and the Book of Mormon, Rosa told us of an experience she had just last night. After we had stopped by to ask her if she wanted to start the missionary discussions again, Rosa went into her room and got ready for bed. Rosa said the spirit she had felt during our visit left, and she felt as if the light in her heart went out. A horrible blackness surrounded her, and her faith failed her. Rosa tried

praying, but the peace she craved still did not come. Then she saw the Church literacy manual, and she picked it up. As Rosa paged through the book and read what little she could, she felt a beautiful calmness. She explained to us that for her that book contains the word of God. And those simple words—"Dios e ama" and "teme a Dios"—filled her soul.[4]

Another teacher-servant who fills me with admiration is Henry Gradillas, a BYU graduate and the principal of Birmingham High School, a few miles north of Los Angeles. He made the school safe, got rid of gangs, improved the curriculum, and forced students to make long-range plans. He's a tough principal. He used to be a captain in the army and he still talks like one. Everybody in his school knows his motto: "You break the rules and you're outta here." When people ask about due process, he says, "Yes, we have it. Sometimes it lasts about two seconds, but we have it."

Before he was at Birmingham, he was principal at Garfield High School in East Los Angeles, where the calculus teacher, Jaime Escalante, took the total number of advanced placement students in calculus from 56 to 336 within five years. You may have seen the movie *Stand and Deliver;* that was Harry Gradillas's school. He says it's the adults who fudge on the rules. Students want them, need them, and understand why they're necessary. For instance, he established a rule that there would be no fights. None. Zero. Zip. Nobody believed he could make it stick because they didn't think there was a way to keep the Latinos from fighting, including the girls. Well, Gradillas is a Latino himself and he thinks a rule has to be applied to everyone to be fair. So he made it stick. When you ask students at Birmingham what happens if they get in a fight, they all give you the same answer. They snap their fingers and tell you, "You're outta here."

At Garfield, Gradillas knew he had to get rid of the gangs. Fourteen of them were terrorizing the school. He gave the teachers a dress code and said, "You're in charge of enforcing the rules."

He told the teachers to stand in front of their classroom doors five minutes before the bell rang, greet each student who entered, and be sure that no one was left in the hall. He gave the administrators walkie-talkies so that everyone had instant communication. He trimmed the bushes in front of his window so he could see what the kids were doing on the school grounds. And it worked.

But the most important thing he did was to set high standards for the students. In the United States of America, he points out, people do not apply for college or for jobs in Spanish. Therefore, all students will speak, read, and write English. Naturally, not all students adore him, not all teachers subscribe to his views, and not all parents agree with his philosophy of education. But at least they know what it is.

I've gone into a lot of detail about Henry Gradillas's background because somebody who loves education and sees its potential for making miracles has to be a hero of mine. But the point I'm getting at is that literacy is literally his way to make love visible. He loves students, and he serves them by helping them be better people.

"All along," says Gradillas, "I have tried to convince educators that it doesn't do any good to give students a *false* sense of self-esteem, which is exactly what happens when you give kids A's in remedial math and then send them out into the real world. That's when you wreck a kid's self-esteem.

"No one can give a student self-esteem; you give people human worth by giving them something worthy of self-esteem."

Then he illustrated this point with a story about his students at Garfield. They had a rule that all of the students had to make paper jackets for their books to keep them clean, but the semester when all entering students were required to take algebra—a first at that school—the kids just wouldn't cover their algebra books. They got scolded, punished, and stood over while they made book jackets, but the jackets just disappeared. Finally, Gradillas "realized that this was a matter of pride. They were in algebra, and they wanted the world to know it. So, we got them plastic covers for these books. And every time I saw a student set his books down, you know what book was always on top? The algebra book. Now, *that's* giving kids self-esteem."[5]

Nobody could say Henry Gradillas is sentimental. But I see so much love in what he is doing. Like Sister Seiter in Guatemala, he is choosing the path of increasing literacy skills as an act of service and of love.

I hope we've been able to think, with a light touch and a fresh perspective, about the serious matter of being literate that asks for the attention of us all. I'm asking us all to think of ways to become lifelong learners so that we can tap into the never-ending pleasure of learning—whether it's a new stitch in crochet or a career change or how to communicate with a grandson. I'm hoping we will remember how the Savior loves us, yearns for us to learn of him, come to him, and follow him. I pray that we will learn so deeply and so well that we will be able, with the psalmist, to read the signs of God's love all around us—for:

> The heavens declare the glory of God; and the firmament sheweth his handywork.
>
> Day unto day uttereth speech, and night unto night sheweth knowledge.
>
> There is no speech nor language, where their voice is not heard.
>
> Their line is gone out through all the earth, and their words to the end of the world. (Psalm 19:1–4)

I pray that we may become literate in the ways that count the most.

11

THANKSGIVING: TO HOLD IN REMEMBRANCE

What is the connection between remembering and thanksgiving?

We get some insight on this question from a wonderful Peanuts cartoon. Linus, Schroeder, and Lucy are just completing the baseball season. Linus suggests that they ought to honor Charlie Brown's dedication as their team manager by giving him a testimonial dinner. Lucy looks dubious and says, "Do you think he really deserves a whole dinner? How about a testimonial snack?" Well, when it comes to giving thanks, I think we should have the whole feast—turkey, pumpkin pie, and the works. I have several ideas to share about remembrance and thanksgiving.

First, remembering the Lord is a commandment. We are commanded to remember the Lord, for the very good reason that when we remember God it is nearly always with an increase of gratitude toward him. There is a beautiful passage in Psalm 103 in which the believer reminds himself, "Bless the Lord, O my soul, and forget not all his benefits." Then the person enumerates some of these benefits that the Lord grants:

Who forgiveth all thine iniquities; who healeth all thy diseases;

Who redeemeth thy life from destruction; who crowneth thee with lovingkindness and tender mercies;

Who satisfieth thy mouth with good things; so that thy youth is renewed like the eagle's. . . .

The Lord is merciful and gracious, slow to anger, and plenteous in mercy. (Psalm 103:2–5, 8)

Aren't these some of the feelings we have as we think about how the Lord has blessed and helped us?

Elaine Cannon, a former general president of the Young Women, talked directly about her concern that she individually and we as a people might be breaking this important commandment. She said:

I have been struck with a mighty fear that I've lived so long without expressing proper gratitude for all that I have, for all that *we* have—for the places we enjoy while we learn our lessons, for the comforts that come to us when we're stricken with sadness, for the fantastic support that this [gospel] system gives us, for the guidance of God, and the direction and comfort and sustaining influence and witness that is ours of the Holy Spirit.[1]

Second, we need to show our appreciation in some way. One of the things I love about children is how candid and honest they are. Here are some letters from children to God that simply bubble over with appreciation and compliments. First is a letter from a little boy: "Dear God, Count me in. Your friend, Herbie." A little girl writes, "Dear God, If I was God I wouldn't be as good at it. Keep it up. Michelle." And here's a real fan letter from another little girl: "You are one of my two favorite men in the world. Patti." And the last letter is from a concerned pet owner who writes: "Dear God. Last week it rained three days. We thought it would be like Noah's Ark but it wasn't. I'm glad because you could only take two of things, remember, and we have three cats. Donna."[2] Don't you think Donna will always remember her feeling of gratitude when she realized she didn't have to decide which cat to leave behind? When was the last time you wrote a thank-you note to God, or offered a prayer in which you didn't ask for anything but simply expressed your gratitude?

I was touched by the story of Marie Lundstrom Gustavson, whose gratitude remained constant for more than sixty years. When she was a fourteen-year-old girl in the late 1920s, she learned about the gospel in Sweden, joined the Church after a year's investigation, and later came to live in Salt Lake City. At a reunion of the Swedish missionaries, she learned the whereabouts of one elder, Henry E. Erickson, who had appealed to her grandmother's kind heart because he was brand new and couldn't speak any Swedish. He was living near Rexburg, Idaho.

She always remembered him, even though home duties kept her occupied. Then finally, in May 1990, sixty-three years after her baptism, she got in touch with Elder Erickson, and she and her husband drove to Idaho to meet him. She thanked him for teaching her the gospel and baptizing her.[3]

Merrill Jenkins was my missionary, and I have the impression that I was the only person he baptized on his mission. After he was dead, his wife told me that he always included me in his prayers, thanking the Lord that he had had a role to play in bringing me into the Church. And you can imagine how I feel about Elder Jenkins!

Is it ever too late to say "Thank you"? No, and I don't think we can say it too often, either, if that is what is in our hearts.

Third, gratitude toward God also increases our gratitude toward other people. When you remember God and his dealings in your life, if you're like me, you feel grateful. When our hearts are filled with gratitude, we don't remember God with fear or with indifference or with a nagging feeling that there's something else on our chore list that we haven't gotten to yet. No, we feel grateful to God for his mercy, and for his loving kindness, and for his generosity to us. And this sense of gratitude and thanksgiving to God spills over into feelings of gratitude and appreciation for others.

Doesn't Thanksgiving make you feel a great desire to show appreciation to those around you? I know it makes me feel like that. My husband, Ed, was one of the most appreciative people I've ever known. Daily he expressed his appreciation to me and to the boys, and the boys in turn grew up acting in the same way. Even when my boys were teenagers, traditionally a heedless time, they always thanked me after a meal. All the effort of cooking became worth it because of their thankful hearts.

Fourth, gratitude is an attitude. Sometimes we don't feel particularly grateful. Often this is because of our circumstances, but I truly testify that circumstances are less important than attitudes. I once read an allegory by Henry Ward Beecher that I used to put in the school newsletter each November for the other teachers and administrators. He wrote: "If one should give me a dish of sand, and tell me there were particles of iron in it, I might look for them with my eyes, and search for them with my clumsy fingers, and be unable to detect them; but let me take a magnet and sweep through it, and how it will draw to itself the almost invisible particles by the mere power of attraction. The thankless heart, like my finger in the sand, discovers no mercies; but let the thankful heart sweep through the day; and as the magnet finds the iron, so it will find, in every hour, some heavenly blessings."

I think what he's saying is that thankfulness is an attitude that depends, to a great extent, on our ability to look at our days with the eyes of thankfulness and to remember God in our daily activities.

Did you know that the better in math you are, the happier you are. Why? Because you're an expert at counting your blessings. Sometimes it's hard to keep the attitude of gratitude when adversity strikes or when life seems overwhelming to us. I read the story of an old missionary couple from a Protestant denomination who had been working in Africa for many years and were returning to New York City to retire in the early years of the twentieth century.

With no pension and broken in health, they were discouraged, fearful of the future.

They happened to be booked on the same ship as Teddy Roosevelt, who was returning from a big-game hunting expedition. They watched the passengers trying to glimpse the great man, the crew fussing over him. . . .

At the dock in New York a band was waiting to greet the President. . . . But the missionary couple slipped off the ship unnoticed.

That night, in a cheap flat they found on the East Side, the man's spirit broke. He said to his wife, "I can't take this; God is not treating us fairly." His wife suggested he go into his bedroom and tell the Lord.

A short time later he came out of the bedroom with a face completely changed. His wife asked, "Dear, what happened?"

"The Lord settled it with me," he said. "I told him how bitter I was that the President should receive this tremendous homecoming, when no one met us when we returned home. And when I finished, it seemed as if the Lord put his hand on my shoulder and said, 'But you're not home yet.'"[4]

Do you think that change in perspective made the old missionary feel differently about God and his relationship to him? Did he feel an increase in thanksgiving and rejoicing in this remembrance of God's love?

I think of appreciation as a kind of faith, because it takes a special kind of perspective to have a grateful heart and to see how gratitude brings us into relationships with God and with each other. There's a wonderful scripture in the Doctrine and Covenants in which the Lord exhorted the Saints of our own day:

Do these things with thanksgiving, with . . . a glad heart and a cheerful countenance—

[And] verily I say, that inasmuch as ye do this, the fulness of the earth is yours, the beasts of the field and the fowls of the air, and that which climbeth upon the trees and walketh upon the earth;

Yea, and the herb, and the good things which come of the earth, whether for food or for raiment, or for houses, or for barns, or for orchards, or for gardens, or for vineyards;

Yea, all things which come of the earth, in the season thereof, are made for the benefit and the use of [all of you], both to please the eye and to gladden the heart;

Yea, for food and for raiment, for taste and for smell, to strengthen the body and to enliven the soul.

And it pleaseth God that he hath given all these things unto [you]; for unto this end were they made. . . .

And in nothing doth [one] offend God, or against none is his wrath kindled, save those who confess not his hand in all things, and obey not his commandments. (D&C 59:15–21)

Well, that's pretty comprehensive, isn't it? I've always thought that there is great wisdom in confessing the Lord's hand in all things, even in our troubles. And I'll tell you why. Gratitude is a way of sharpening our vision without putting on glasses. For one thing, it requires us to think about our lives in a new way. It requires us to think about our lives in the presence of God, because gratitude has to be expressed, and that means we step outside of our own perspective to see things from God's perspective.

For another thing, we may feel afraid or worried or upset about many things in our lives, but seeing in them a reason for gratitude readjusts those feelings. We feel more confident, less afraid, and happier. In fact, there's nothing like thanking the Lord for a problem to make me start laughing. And once I've laughed at a problem, it never has the same power over me.

Now, it takes a little practice to develop an attitude of appreciation. Let me give you an example. A couple of years ago, I took my older son with me on an expedition into the sugar-cane plantation on the big island of Hawaii where I grew up, back to the village that we lived in. The village has been deserted for years, and most of the buildings are gone. Only the foundation remains where our house once stood, but the natural features of the landscape are unchanged.

In one of the places on the old lava flow that had hit the beach, there was a hole in the rocks, going down a few feet into the water. Somehow my father had discovered that lobsters lived there. I remember how my mother would say, "Let's have lobster for dinner," two or three times a week, and I would say, "Oh, no! Not again!" Just goes to show you how much children know.

Dad would bait a line and drop it into the hole and presto! a lobster would take the bait. He would snatch it up and put in his basket, repeating the process until he had enough, usually about four or five lobsters for our family. My mother would have the water boiling in the big pan on the stove when we got back. We'd drop the lobsters in, cook them, and then take them out and eat them—not with butter but with soy sauce. Yum, yum!

If we'd had a line and some bait and a way to cook them, I think Ken and I would have tried fishing for lobster on the spot. My mouth still waters when I think of how delicious that taste was. But from my child's perspective, fresh lobster was nothing special—nothing, for instance, like canned peaches. Now *those* were special!

Let me encourage you to thank the Lord for the lobsters in your life, even if they seem like the dullest, most routine, least exciting lobsters in the world. I guarantee that you will begin to see them more deliciously.

Fifth, we can learn more about memory and thanksgiving by studying the scriptures. I spent some time looking up some scriptures about memory, forgetting, and remembrance. There's a long string of negative admonitions, when the Lord reminds people that they have sinned and forgotten him or turned away from him, but there are also some lovely scriptures that remind us to hold

Christ and our Heavenly Father in remembrance and remind us that they hold us in their remembrance.

Psalm 97:12 says, "Rejoice in the Lord, ye righteous; and give thanks at the remembrance of his holiness." To me, this scripture says that *because* the Lord is holy, we can safely trust in him and rely upon him. We know that we are cherished in the arms of his love, not because we are particularly holy, but because he is. And this is a blessing to us.

The prophet Jeremiah speaks of how the Lord covenants with the house of Israel in a way that the covenant cannot be forgotten. He says:

> But this shall be the covenant that I will make with the house of Israel; After those days, saith the Lord, I will put my law in their inward parts, and write it in their hearts; and will be their God, and they shall be my people.
>
> And they shall teach no more every man his neighbour, and every man his brother, saying, Know the Lord: for they shall all know me, from the least of them unto the greatest of them, saith the Lord: for I will forgive their iniquity, and I will remember their sin no more.
>
> Thus saith the Lord, which giveth the sun for a light by day, and the ordinances of the moon and of the stars for a light by night, which divideth the sea when the waves thereof roar; The Lord of hosts is his name. (Jeremiah 31:33–35)

I love this scripture because it seems very relevant to my childhood, growing up in Hawaii. When we're not in the cities, we become very aware of the stars and the moon, how they mark and give direction to the darkest night. Even in the cities, we are always aware of the ocean ringing us around in every direction. We know and have suffered through its power when "the waves thereof roar." We understand how small and helpless we are against its might, so when we think of God as someone who can divide that sea, we know we are in the presence of real power.

But the point of this scripture is the power of covenants over memory. When the Lord says he will instill this covenant upon our hearts so that it cannot be forgotten, he goes on to say that the covenant will be so instilled in every fiber of our being that we will not even need to teach each other about the Lord anymore, because each and every one of us will know him in our hearts.

I would compare this to the situation of coming to you and saying, "There's someone I'd like you to meet. Here she is," and it turns out to be your mother. You'd exclaim, "You don't need to tell me about her. I *know* her." Wouldn't it be wonderful to have a heart filled with love for the Lord just as our hearts are filled with love for our mothers? Most of us could talk for hours, just sharing memories of our mothers. Wouldn't it be wonderful if we could all talk for hours just sharing memories of our experiences with our Father in Heaven and with Jesus and the wonderful experiences we have had—the answers to prayers, the feelings of being loved and cherished by them, and the direction that has come into our lives when we needed it? Well, that's the promise of the Lord to people who make covenants with all their hearts and keep them with full diligence of spirit.

It interests me that this scripture, which talks about how we will always remember the Lord, also talks about how the Lord forgets—and praises him for forgetting. That's because, when we are willing to repent and exercise faith, it's our sins and iniquities that he forgets, out of his boundless charity and his willingness to help us make the Atonement operational in our lives. "I will forgive their iniquity," says the Lord, "and I will remember their sin no more." Isn't that a wonderful promise, something that we can be eternally grateful for?

So if you want a wonderful Thanksgiving experience, try reading the scriptures looking for stories and passages about remembering the Lord and having grateful hearts.

Sixth, the core of our worship service is an act of remembering. I am always so grateful to take the sacrament, because of the opportunity that it gives us with that thimbleful of water and that

123

tiny piece of bread to remember Jesus and what he did for us. Do you pay attention to the sacrament prayers, which ask our Heavenly Father "to bless and sanctify this bread to the souls of all those who partake of it; that they may eat in remembrance of the body of thy Son . . ." (D&C 20:77), and the parallel passage in the blessing on the water?

What is it that we're supposed to remember? Yes, we remember Christ's atonement for our sins and his death on the cross, but I also like to remember the intimate setting in the upper chamber where he instituted the sacrament, where he took ordinary bread and broke it into pieces and passed it to his apostles and talked to them while they chewed it, concentrating on what he was saying and trying to understand.

> And he took bread, and gave thanks, and brake it, and gave unto them, saying, This is my body which is given for you: this do in remembrance of me.
> Likewise also the cup after supper, saying, This cup is the new testament in my blood, which is shed for you. (Luke 22:19–20)

That account was written by Luke, who was not present in person. We weren't present in person either, but what would it have been like to be in that upper room, to hear the Savior's voice, to take the bread from his hand, to hear him say, "This do in remembrance of me," as though he were already gone but while we could still see him before our eyes? When we remember, he *is* there before us, able to nourish us as if with bread, explaining to us in words that are simple but that we sometimes have to ponder hard to understand.

So when we take the sacrament, let us recognize it as an act of memory, a deed that we perform in the present to allow a memory to become real and vivid within us so that the covenants we renew and commit to live by will be a source of gratitude for us.

Seventh, one of the gifts for which we can be most grateful is the Holy Ghost. I think it's important that a primary function of the Holy Ghost is to help us remember. Jesus told his apostles on that same night of the Passover and the Last Supper, "But the Comforter, which is the Holy Ghost, whom the Father will send in my name, he shall teach you all things, and bring all things to your remembrance, whatsoever I have said unto you" (John 14:26).

I believe that the things he can bring to our remembrance are not just the words of the scriptures, important though they are, but also the words that he has spoken directly to us, to our hearts and to our minds. The Lord told Oliver Cowdery, when he was seeking personal revelation:

> Verily, verily, I say unto you, if you desire a further witness, cast your mind upon the night that you cried unto me in your heart, that you might know concerning the truth of these things.
>
> Did I not speak peace to your mind concerning the matter? What greater witness can you have than from God?
>
> And now, behold, you have received a witness; for if I have told you things which no man knoweth have you not received a witness? (D&C 6:22–24)

You have heard the voice of the Lord at some time in the past and in some manner, speaking to your mind or to your heart, giving you a feeling, an impression, or a whisper. When we had hands laid on our heads and received the gift of the Holy Ghost, we received the promise of memory. I believe that we can remember sacred experiences that we have had with our Heavenly Father and with the Savior, and that such memories will help us with present adversities. And we need to share our testimonies of these things with our families, friends, and brothers and sisters to strengthen the faith of all.

Fran Vetter of Puyallup, Washington, wrote of an experience she had in listening to the Holy Ghost. Her mother-in-law was spending the afternoon with her and the children; she'd been ill for several years, but she seemed extremely "healthy and vibrant" that afternoon and urged Fran to run a few errands. Fran, who hadn't seen her this strong for several years, was grateful for the chance to get some of her own work done and drove away, but at the first stop light, she heard someone say, "Go back home now!" She looked around and saw no one. So, despite the urgent feeling that accompanied the words, she drove on. Within seconds, the warning came again. This time she did not ignore it but returned home immediately.

When she got home, everything seemed fine. Her mother-in-law was enjoying watching the children, who were absorbed in a cartoon program; everything was quiet. Fran felt confused as she explained that she'd changed her mind. She sat down, feeling bewildered, and just then her daughter exclaimed, "Look, Mom, Grandma is making funny faces." Fran saw that her mother-in-law's face had turned a dusky blue and was contorting in spasms. She was having a grand mal seizure.

Quickly Fran helped her to the floor and called the paramedics. Although they came within minutes and stabilized her, she was hospitalized for a long time and did not fully recover. Almost certainly she would have died, alone with the children, if Fran had not returned.[5] Do you think Fran was grateful for the whisperings of the Holy Ghost, and grateful also for the past experiences she had had to make that voice a living reality in her memory?

Just to summarize, then, we've talked about seven ideas about memory and gratitude—one for each day of the week. First, remembering the Lord is a commandment. Second, we need to show our appreciation in some way. Third, gratitude toward God also increases our gratitude toward other people. Fourth, gratitude is an attitude. Fifth, we can learn more about memory and thanksgiving by studying the scriptures. Sixth, the most important part of our worship service is the sacrament—and the sacrament is an act of remembering. Seventh, one of the gifts for which we can be most grateful is the Holy Ghost.

Let me conclude with the blessing of the apostle Paul upon the Philippian Saints:

> Grace be unto you, and peace, from God our Father, and from the Lord Jesus Christ.
>
> I thank my God upon every remembrance of you, [there's that word again!—remembrance]
>
> Always in every prayer of mine for you all making request with joy,
>
> For your fellowship in the gospel from the first day until now;
>
> Being confident of this very thing, that he which hath begun a good work in you will perform it until the day of Jesus Christ. (Philippians 1:2–6)

May this be our blessing, too—that as members of families, as circles of friends, and as ward members, we will hold each other in remembrance, and that together we can remember Jesus Christ, our beloved Savior, and the good work he is performing in us. I pray that we will all remember that the Lord is our shepherd, that he loves us, and that we will be good undershepherds, giving love and care to those we come in contact with. I pray that we will have hearts quick to remember and slow to forget, and that as a result of our remembrance we will have hearts filled with gratitude.

CHRISTMAS EXTRAVAGANCE

I've titled this chapter "Christmas Extravagance" because Christmas seems to be a time of delicious, glorious abundance, profusion, and excess—a real cornucopia of a time. I realized I felt this way about it as I listened to one of those presentations I'm sure we've all heard—about how you have to deal with the stress of the holidays by setting priorities, establishing limits, making yes-lists and no-lists, deciding what you'll eat and what you won't, working out a budget, a schedule, a plan. It all sounded very prudent, moderate, controlled, restrained. It all sounded very boring. It sounded like no fun at all.

Yet I realized that it made good sense, and I know that the Christmas season is ruined for some people by bingeing—they spend too much, eat too much, do too much, run too fast and too hard. They end up feeling sad, selfish, and sinful. So how could I actually want extravagance? Isn't that awfully reckless and foolish of me?

I began thinking about where this idea of mine might have come from, and I realized it comes from thirty-three years in elementary school. Sometimes we complain that Christmas seems to start in the middle of November. Well, in elementary school, Christmas actually starts the week before Halloween. Remember that second-grade feeling when you got to magically transform your identity into that of a fairy princess or a cowboy and go out after dark to the homes of perfect strangers and chant some strange words like "trick or treat" and they would pour candy into your bag? If that's not plenitude, what is? And the grown-ups who are always saying "We can't afford it" or "You haven't earned it" or "Have you been a good girl or boy?" aren't asking any of those questions. They're just smiling at you and laughing with you and praising your magic wand or your furry chaps and dishing out the candy some more. Do you remember that second-grade feeling?

And then comes Thanksgiving, which has something to do with people in funny hats carrying guns with bell-shaped muzzles and turkeys and Indians and America but mostly being very thankful and grateful for all our blessings and going over the river and through the woods to Grandmother's house.

And then comes Christmas, the red-and-green holiday, with trees and strings of popcorn and the incredibly delicious power of knowing that you're making a present for your mom and dad and it's your secret and they don't even know about it because you're doing it at school. And there are treats and Santa Claus and Christmas carols and people making wishes like "Merry Christmas," and that's magic, too, like "trick or treat" but somehow even better.

And you don't find out about it at school, but there's a baby—baby Jesus—who is an important part of Christmas, and a stable with a donkey with furry ears and a cow with gentle eyes, and the wise men in splendid costumes with the glamorous camels, and Mary and Joseph and the shepherds holding lambs and wonderful crooks. But they're all looking at the baby, and on their faces is an expression that makes you feel a little funny inside. It's a peaceful, thoughtful expression that brings stillness, even in the midst of the blinking lights and the ho-ho-ho's and the "Merry Christmases." And so you look at the baby too, and a little of the stillness comes into your own heart. And somehow you remember the baby, even while the presents get deeper under the tree and some of them have *your* name on them, and you help your mom make the gingerbread house and you get to make shingles on the roof out of those nasty pink wafers that you wouldn't touch at any other time of the year but somehow, they taste like Christmas.

And so, I have to tell you that I have a very second-grade approach to Christmas. It's the culmination of three important months in a child's life that start with an experience of transformation into someone special and an outpouring of grace—candy, not because you've earned it but just because you are—and then continue with a linking of hardship and thankfulness and culminate at the darkest time of the year in a festival of lights, music, singing, and jolly Santas with more gifts. And that baby. Don't forget that baby.

So I'm not very sympathetic with the yes-lists and the no-lists. And it's not just because they don't sound very much like fun. It's because they don't sound very much like joy. If it's true that you can never get enough of what you don't need, then maybe it's also true that you can never give too much of what you have in plenty.

Let's think about extravagance for Christmas. Think about the plenteousness of Christmas—its abundance, copiousness, liberality, bounty, lavishness, exuberance, luxuriance, profusiveness; its unstinted, unmeasured, inexhaustible plenty. What can we be extravagant with? What do we have in abundance?

Let me name a few things just to get you started. We all have an absolutely unlimited supply of smiles. Sometimes we save them just for the family. Or worse, sometimes we save them just for the people at work. Well, they are *not* in short supply! Let's start passing them out, one per every pair of eyes we look into with a few left over so that we can catch ourselves smiling even when we're alone.

Something else that we've all got in unlimited abundance is a supply of greetings. "Merry Christmas!" If you think about it, it's a wonderful greeting. It's not just the marker of a day or a season, but it's a profound wish for a certain quality, that this day or this season will be marked by the quality of a merry heart, one so full of happiness that it spills over into laughter and delight. Every time you wish someone a "Merry Christmas" it's like a personal vote for that person's delight and happiness.

You also have an unlimited fountain of song springing up. Don't you just thrill to the exuberance and beauty of Christmas carols? It's fun and easy to sing at Christmas. Every radio, every department store, every supermarket fills the air with seasonal songs. You may not like all of them, but you have good feelings about most of them because they are, after all, connected to Christmas, that time of superabundance. A song weighs nothing and takes up absolutely no storage space. It sounds better if you sing it out loud, but it doesn't mind singing away all by itself in your heart while you're on a crowded elevator or sitting in the world's slowest-moving meeting. It improves immeasurably if you sing it with someone else, especially a child, and it doesn't matter where it ends—even in the middle of the third verse when you can't remember what line comes next—as long as you laugh about it.

Now, I happen to think that Christmas music fits any time of the year. I really enjoy requesting "Far, Far Away on Judea's Plains" as a rest song when I go out on assignments—not only because I enjoy the song but also because I enjoy the startled looks on people's faces when I ask for this song in the middle of August. But I also think that one of the most wonderful things about singing at Christmas is that all music seems to fit the season. If you want to sing "Jingle Bells," that's great. If you want to sing "Shine On, Harvest Moon," that's a reminder about the bounties the Lord has blessed us with. If you want to sing "Popcorn Popping on the Apricot Tree," it's a signal of the hope we have in Christ. I think it *all* fits.

But some of the most beautiful Christian music ever written was written for this season of the year. One of the new songs I learned as an adult—and it's not a traditional carol at all—is called "'Twas in the Moon of Winter Time." It was written to the tune of an old French carol during the early seventeenth century by Father Jean de Brebeuf. Father de Brebeuf was a Jesuit missionary who worked among the Huron Indians in Canada (he died in 1649), and he wrote this carol to tell the story of baby Jesus to them in a language and with images they could understand.

This carol is extremely meaningful to me because, as a Japanese Buddhist, I always experienced Christmas as a borrowed holiday. There are no Japanese Christmas carols. There are no Buddhist Christmas carols. But for people like me, the many mansions of the gospel have open doors to accept us in our diversity and to welcome us in and give us a place at the table and a stocking under the tree. I cannot think of Christmas without thinking of the many people who generously translated the holiday into terms that I could understand, first as a little Buddhist girl, then as a shy new convert trying to understand Mormonism, then as a Hawaiian transplanted to Utah with its snow and lighted street decorations. I do not know Father de Brebeuf, but I am thankful in my heart to him for rewriting the Christmas story into Huron to open the doors of that miracle time to them. Because of his act of compassion, he has the honor of having written the first Canadian Christmas carol and perhaps the first carol in the New World.[1]

'Twas in the moon of wintertime when all the
   leaves had fled
The mighty Gitchee Manitou sent angel
   choirs instead.
Before their light the stars grew dim,
And wandering hunters heard the hymn:
(Chorus)
Jesus, your king, is born. Jesus is born.
In excelsis gloria!

The earliest moon of wintertime was not so
   round and fair

As was the ring of glory on the helpless infant
   there.
While chiefs from far before him knelt,
With gifts of fox and beaver pelt
(Chorus)
Jesus, your king, is born. Jesus is born.
In excelsis gloria!

O children of the forest free, O sons of
   Manitou
The holy child of earth and heaven is born
   this day for you.
Come kneel before the radiant boy,
Who brings you beauty, peace and joy,
(Chorus)
Jesus, your king, is born. Jesus is born.
In excelsis gloria!

This song makes me think of the scripture, "For behold, the Lord doth grant unto all nations, of their own nation and tongue, to teach his word, yea, in wisdom, all that he seeth fit that they should have" (Alma 29:8).

Let's look at what else you have to give for Christmas. You have time. Even though you may think that time is what you have in shortest supply, you have all the time there is, all the time in the world, the morning and the evening, the day that God has made for us to rejoice and be glad in. Think of it not as a machine to be used for maximum efficiency, but as a gift to be given with open hands and an open heart.

You also have an unlimited number of prayers to offer during this season. You can pray for the people in the hospital as you drive by. You can pray for the policeman directing traffic after the basketball game. You can pray for the person you see on the news whose face and plight touch you, even if you see her face only in a crowd. You can pray for the clerk in the shoe store, for the

Salvation Army bell ringer, for the grandchild in Florida, for the president of the United States, for the person standing in the detergent aisle trying to make up her mind what soap to buy. And this doesn't even begin to touch the hundreds of people you know personally for whom you can pray.

Think of the power of that prayer. It's as if you lift someone with loving hands and hold him or her up in remembrance before God. That person is in your memory, in your heart, in your thoughts. And now you have brought his or her name before God in joyous, sympathetic remembrance. What a wonderful gift of plenitude!

Now, perhaps you're thinking, "But some of these people are strangers. I don't even know them. I don't know if they need my prayers. I don't know if my prayers will do them any good." That's not the point. You're not praying for them because *they* need it. You're praying for them because *you* have a prayer to give. The prayer does not exist because of their poverty. It exists because of your richness.

And think what it means that *you* have this inexhaustible treasury of benevolence and bounty. Why, it means that you're rich, wealthy, overflowing with abundance! You can lavish it, squander it. It doesn't matter. You can never give so much that you'll run out.

Think of the Christmas story. Isn't one of the things we love about it the absolute feast or famine that characterizes it? Mary and Joseph were not only poor but homeless, not only away from their families but totally thrown on the mercy of strangers. These are extreme circumstances—extravagantly bad circumstances. The visitors who came to see the Christ child were not moderately well-off, moderately respectable, or cautiously optimistic. They were the extremes of society—poor shepherds and gorgeously appareled kings bearing fabulous gifts. The shepherds did not take a vote, arrange a sheep-watching schedule, and come to the stable when it was light enough to walk comfortably on the road. They left their flocks and came with haste in the darkness of night. God did not send a neatly typed heavenly memo to the religious and theological leaders of the day, but a multitude of angels filled the sky and the night with their song of glory and rejoicing.

Do you have faith that you can give to someone? This someone may feel that God is far away. But remember, you are not giving the gift because he or she needs it but because you have it to give.

Do you have a compliment to give someone out of your treasurehouse of appreciation? Do you have forgiveness to give out of your own rich sense of the Father's endless mercy?

Did you get ideas from President Howard W. Hunter's 1994 Christmas devotional speech about your richness? He said:

> This Christmas, mend a quarrel. Seek out a forgotten friend. Dismiss suspicion and replace it with trust. Write a letter. Give a soft answer. Encourage youth. Manifest your loyalty in word and deed. Keep a promise. Forego a grudge. Forgive an enemy. Apologize. Try to understand. Examine your demands on others. Think first of someone else. Be kind. Be gentle. Laugh a little more. Express your gratitude. Welcome a stranger. Gladden the heart of a child. Take pleasure in the beauty and wonder of the earth. Speak your love and speak it again. Christmas is a celebration, and there is no celebration that compares with the realization of its true meaning—with the sudden stirring of the heart that has extended itself unselfishly in the things that matter most.[2]

What do you have to give? The keys to God's storehouse are in your hands. You are richer than Midas. Think about your abundance! What extravagant gift can you give this Christmas out of your bounty?

"Give," said Jesus, "and it shall be given unto you; good measure, pressed down, and shaken together, and running over" (Luke 6:38). And how did Jesus give? Listen to what Paul says, and to how extravagantly he says it:

135

God loveth a cheerful giver.

And God is able to make all grace abound toward you; that ye, always having all sufficiency in all things, may abound to every good work:

(As it is written, He hath dispersed abroad; he hath given to the poor: his righteousness remaineth for ever.

Now he that ministereth seed to the sower both minister bread for your food, and multiply your seed sown, and increase the fruits of your righteousness;)

Being enriched in every thing to all bountifulness, which causeth through us thanksgiving to God.

For the administration of this service not only supplieth the want of the saints, but is abundant also by many thanksgivings unto God . . . for the exceeding grace of God in you.

Thanks be unto God for his unspeakable gift. (2 Corinthians 9:7–12, 14–15)

You are the heir of eternity. All that the Father hath is yours. Can his storehouse ever be empty? There is no scarcity or rationing or restriction. When he pours out blessings, he opens the windows of heaven, and we cannot contain what he showers upon us. We are infinitely precious to him, infinitely loved, infinitely cherished. You can never give away too much of what cannot be exhausted in you—the inexhaustible, unstinted love of God.

Bursting out of the tiny package we call Christmas, I pray for all of us the merry heart that comes with Merry Christmas, the cheerful giving that God loves, the overflowing faith, the plenitude of hope, and an eternity of charity.

13

"NOTHING SHALL BE IMPOSSIBLE"

Throughout the year are sprinkled days of new beginnings. The first day of school, the starting of spring, the beginning of the year, the first day of a diet or a reading program or any new venture is a time of beginnings, a time for wiping out dissatisfactions and failures of the past, a time for taking stock and renewing priorities, and a time of looking forward to the future with hope. Any day we choose to make a new beginning is a day when we can draw strength from the Lord's promise, "Nothing shall be impossible."

This phrase appears twice in the scriptures, both times in the New Testament. The first time it is used as part of the angel's message to Mary. When the angel first told her she would bear a child, Mary asked: "How shall this be, seeing I know not a man?"

And the angel answered and said unto her, The Holy Ghost shall come upon thee, and the power of the Highest shall overshadow thee: therefore also that holy thing which shall be born of thee shall be called the Son of God.

And, behold, thy cousin Elisabeth, she hath also conceived a son in her old age: and this is the sixth month with her, who was called barren.

For with God nothing shall be impossible.

And Mary said, Behold the handmaid of the Lord; be it unto me according to thy word. And the angel departed from her. (Luke 1:34–38; emphasis added)

The second time this phrase is used occurs during Jesus' ministry. As Jesus was teaching, a man came and knelt before him and said:

Lord, have mercy on my son: for he is lunatick, and sore vexed: for ofttimes he falleth into the fire, and oft into the water.

And I brought him to thy disciples, and they could not cure him.

Then Jesus answered and said, O faithless and perverse generation, how long shall I be with you? how long shall I suffer you? bring him hither to me.

And Jesus rebuked the devil; and he departed out of him: and the child was cured from that very hour.

Then came the disciples to Jesus apart, and said, Why could not we cast him out?

And Jesus said unto them, Because of your unbelief: for verily I say unto you, If ye have faith as a grain of mustard seed, ye shall say unto this mountain, Remove hence to yonder place; and it shall remove; *and nothing shall be impossible unto you.*

Howbeit this kind goeth not out but by prayer and fasting. (Matthew 17:14–21; emphasis added)

Now, let's look for a moment at the similarities and the differences between these two passages. In the first passage, an angel is speaking to Mary, reassuring her that the amazing message he has given her is true, and that "with God" nothing is impossible. Mary then accepts the angel's message and her mission, whereupon the angel departs. I think it is significant that the angel "departs." It would have been so much easier for Mary if the angel had just stayed around. That way, when the whispers began about her pregnancy and when Joseph was coming to the conclusion that she had been unfaithful to him during their betrothal period, she could have just said, "This angel has a message for you. He'll explain everything." But it doesn't happen that way. True, the angel returns once more to reassure Joseph as well, but only when matters are at the very point of crisis and Joseph has made the decision to divorce Mary. Once Mary made the choice and accepted her mission, then Mary had to find the strength to fulfill it.

In the second case, we have Jesus' disciples failing to cast an evil spirit out of a child. Jesus is very seldom impatient with his disciples, but he seems to be in this case. He exclaims: "O faithless and perverse generation, how long shall I be with you? how long shall I suffer you?" After he heals the child, he acknowledges to his disciples that this type of evil spirit really is a difficult case that requires the extra effort of fasting and prayer, but he concentrates on what the real problem is: their lack of faith.

If they have enough faith, he encourages them, they can do anything. "Nothing shall be impossible unto you," he says.

Now, did you notice that the angel told Mary that *with God* nothing was impossible, whereas Jesus told his disciples that nothing was impossible *for them* if they would exercise faith? These two statements are not incompatible. It's not because we have enough faith in ourselves that we can do anything; it's because we have enough faith in God that we can expect mountains to move.

Spiritual strength begins with making choices, by saying "yes" to the Lord, as Mary said "yes" to the angel. Then we need to develop personal strength, because the angel will depart from us, and we need to develop that strength by coming unto Christ.

Making Choices

I think it's very significant that the angel who came to Mary didn't just descend in a blaze of light, make his speech, and disappear again. He delivered his message to Mary and then waited. He waited while she asked a question about something she didn't understand. He explained the answer and taught her a gospel principle in the process. And then he waited again. And Mary thought about the message, about the answer to her question, and then she made her decision and said, "Behold the handmaid of the Lord," or in other words, "I am the Lord's servant."

The point is, Mary chose. She made a decision. She exercised her agency. Whatever feelings she may have had of confusion and inadequacy and being overwhelmed, she clearly understood what the mission was that the angel announced to her, and she also understood that in the parts that were impossible for her, nothing was impossible for God.

It is our experiences in mortality that make our decisions real and teach us what we need to learn about freedom. We all make choices. We all make decisions.

We think of choices often in blacks and whites, as choices between good and evil. Choices between good and evil are easy. It's choices between two goods that are hard. Do you know what I mean? I doubt you ever look at the calendar and muse, "Let's see, should I go to homemaking meeting or should I rob a convenience store?" Instead, you choose between good things. You could take the children to the zoo, or pore over catalogues of spring daffodils, or clean out that closet you put on your list of New Year's resolutions.

Mary didn't have to choose between good and evil. Being betrothed to Joseph was a perfectly good option. Being married to Joseph, as would have happened without the visitation of the angel, would have been fine. And there's no question about which choice was going to bring the most intense sorrow, the most social complications, and the most ambiguity into her life. But Mary didn't make her choice on the basis of what would make her life easiest. She made it "according to [God's] word" (Luke 1:38).

Members of the Church who welcome baptism at age eight are making a good choice. People who are converted and baptized later in life are also making a good choice. And all of us who choose to have the experiences that keep our testimonies alive and vibrant continue to make good choices.

140

As Latter-day Saints, we believe that we came into this world with agency. Whatever primal intelligence is, it includes choice. We believe that agency is so important that God is God because he cannot and will not violate our agency. We believe that we can become as God now is because of our agency.

We know how important agency is to our Heavenly Father. He has a respect so profound for it that he will endure seeing us do terrible things to ourselves and to each other rather than override our agency. And how he must rejoice when we use it wisely!

The Strength of Faith

I think one of the reasons the angel left Mary is that she had to be free to work out the consequences of her choice. How much could she have grown in understanding and experience if the angel had stayed right beside her? We need to develop strength *in ourselves*, because the angel will depart from us.

Sometimes we hear the message that our strength is not desirable or wanted. Sometimes women feel that they should defer to others—that their husbands' opinions are more important than their own, that the spiritual living teacher in Relief Society must be more spiritual than they are, or that their needs and wants should be sacrificed to those of their children. Should we retreat to being passive or weak or inadequate because the idea of becoming strong frightens us or someone else?

No healthy marriage needs to fear a strong woman or a strong man in it. Strength is a virtue as long as it is balanced with other strengths. For example, we've talked about the importance of respecting and safeguarding our own agency so that we can make righteous choices. Respect for agency alone, without love, can lead to excessive individualism and selfishness. Love is a wonderful virtue, but if it is not balanced by respect for agency and by faith in the Lord, it can become undisciplined and smothering instead of nurturing.

During the fall of 1992, Sister Michaelene P. Grassli, then

general president of the Primary, and I visited the stakes of Japan and Korea, holding conferences, listening to the sisters and the priesthood leaders, learning from them, and teaching them. This was an assignment that I thought long and prayed hard over. To prepare, I talked to recently returned mission presidents and translators. I contacted Relief Society presidents throughout Japan and Korea, trying to learn the needs of the sisters. I contacted many people who had moved from Japan recently or who had visited in Japan. They all said that the inactivity statistics were alarming— that investigators experienced great joy in learning the gospel and joining the Church, but that within a year or two many of them simply stopped coming.

I tried to understand why, and I think I had an insight into their situation when I read an address by Elder Dallin H. Oaks titled, "Our Strengths Can Become Our Downfall." In it, he explained twenty different categories of behavior in which a commendable strength can, if carried to an extreme, become a stumbling-block to us.[1]

The Japanese culture provides great strengths that work to benefit the Church in Japan. For instance, Japanese people are very hard working. They are proud of doing their best and feel ashamed of failing. They are an obedient people with great respect for authority. You can see how these strengths are real blessings to the Japanese members, but also how they can become weaknesses if carried to excess. For instance, the desire to succeed may mean that someone will not try something new for fear of failing. Respect for authority is a good thing, but we saw Japanese Saints who expected their leaders to be perfect and who quickly became inactive because they could not see their leaders as people who were also learning and growing. On the other hand, we saw leaders who expected immediate and total obedience and who did not always adequately respect the agency of members.

Think about your own family. Think about the strengths of your children and of your spouse. Think about the strengths of those you work with in your Church calling, and also the strengths that you bring to that position and to those relationships. In addition to building our own strengths, can we acknowledge, and honor, and increase the strength of others by encouraging them to grow? My wonderful husband, Ed, valued my strengths and built them up so that I could make progress in ways that simply would not have been possible if my growth had not been important to him.

For example, when Ed was appointed as regional associate commissioner of the Administration on Aging in Denver, we knew we were going to move. I was teaching elementary school in Salt Lake City and hoped to teach school in Denver after we got established, but Ed quietly opened doors for me before we even left Salt Lake City. Cherry Creek School District at that time was a very popular district with good teachers—new schools, adequate funding, and progressive methods. Ed had moved to Denver in March to begin his job while the boys and I stayed in Salt Lake City to finish the school year. I asked Ed if he could get me an interview with the Cherry Creek District. He talked to the personnel director, who said, "Just have her send an application."

Ed explained, "She's going to be here on Friday. Is it possible for her to have an interview?"

The personnel officer repeated, "Just have her send in the application."

But Ed persisted. He talked to someone else—and had no better luck—so he finally asked, "May I speak to the superintendent?" The person said, "There is no superintendent. There's an acting superintendent, Don Stenzel."

So Ed said, "Please let me talk to him."

Well, Don Stenzel said the same thing. "It's awfully difficult. We have only two first-grade positions opening in the district and we have about a thousand applications."

But Ed still persisted, in his gentle way, "You know, I may be prejudiced, but I think you would want to see my wife."

There was a long silence on the other end, and then Ed, who

had been praying during this pause, heard, "All right, send her in at 10:30 on Friday."

So I went in at 10:30 with all my credentials and portfolio and samples of curriculum materials. Don looked through everything and said, "I'm going to take you to the two schools with the openings."

He drove me first to Holly Ridge School, where I had an interview with the principal; then he picked me up and took me to Eastridge, the second school, then took me back to the office and thanked me very much for coming. (I still hadn't filled out an application at this point.)

I came home Sunday evening, and at 8 A.M. on Monday my principal at Indian Hills School said, "There's a call for you from Denver."

I said, "Oh, it must be Ed."

But when I answered the phone, the voice on the other end said, "This is Don Stenzel."

I said, "Oh, thank you so much for all you did for me."

He said, "How does Eastridge sound?"

I asked, "What do you mean?"

He repeated, "How does the job at Eastridge sound?"

I exclaimed, "Are you offering me a job?"

He said, "Yes, we would love to have you take the Eastridge position."

I was breathless but I said, "And I would love to take it."

So he sent me the contract.

Ed gave me the same kind of encouragement and support as a mother, as a wife, and as a Church worker. Calling after calling has made me feel overwhelmed and inadequate, but Ed always reminded me of my strengths and helped me build new strengths. Can we do the same in our families, with our colleagues at work, and with the brothers and sisters with whom we labor in our Church callings?

Remember, even if an angel comes with an invitation to a new experience, and even if we choose to say yes to that experience, the angel will ultimately depart from us and we must have the strength to walk the path that we have chosen.

And of course, we must have faith to walk that path. We have to develop our own faith *in Christ*—not in substitutes for Christ. Even if we have wonderful marriage partners upon whom to rely, even if we have the most devoted and kindly bishops in the world, and even if we have developed much strength in ourselves, our ultimate faith must be in the Savior, not in any human being.

Alma preached powerfully to the people, saying,

> Repent, repent, for the Lord God hath spoken it!
>
> Behold, he sendeth an invitation unto all men [and women], for the arms of mercy are extended toward them, and he saith: Repent, and I will receive you.
>
> Yea, he saith: Come unto me and ye shall partake of the fruit of the tree of life; yea, ye shall eat and drink of the bread and the waters of life freely;
>
> Yea, come unto me and bring forth works of righteousness. . . .
>
> Behold, I say unto you, that the good shepherd doth call you; yea, and in his own name he doth call you, which is the name of Christ. (Alma 5:32–35, 38)

There are many times when we rely on the love, the commitment, and the wisdom of other people. Often our prayers are answered by the ministrations of someone who is sensitive to our needs or to the whisperings of the Spirit. And often, we're the answer to someone else's prayer. But we can't rely on our parents, on our children, on our spouses, or on our Church leaders all the time. Even the apostles, the men closest to Jesus, failed the anxious and loving father of the epileptic child until the father came directly to Jesus, the Son of God.

What does it mean when he asks us to pray to the Father in his name? Sometimes we think that our prayers aren't as good as those offered at stake or general conference, and we forget that our personal prayers are *personal*. They are *very* personal. Think about how you communicate in a personal way with people to whom you feel close. Do you deliver a lecture, as though they were a congregation or a class? Do you think of complicated and formal ways to arrange your sentences? No, you spill out what is in your heart. You ask questions from your heart because you so much want to understand what is in their hearts. You think about a conversation after it has occurred, and often, as soon as you see that friend again, you will immediately continue the discussion from the same point or provide more news, or explain a new insight you have had, or ask a new question about something that you don't understand.

I think that Heavenly Father is pleased with all of our prayers, but I think he is especially pleased when we pray with our whole hearts, when we share ourselves completely without trying to make excuses or to make ourselves look good. Fasting is a way of peeling away things that are constant distractions so that we can temporarily concentrate on our spiritual relationships. Although fasting may bring physical discomfort, I have always loved to fast because it frees what seems like an enormous amount of time that goes into preparing, eating, and cleaning up after a meal. And having this time to pray, meditate, and read the scriptures is a wonderful gift.

Can we approach the Lord as a beloved friend? Can we hunger and thirst for the time that we can spend with our Heavenly Father? Can we go eagerly and with anticipation to our prayers? When we do, our faith will increase, because we will discover that prayer becomes easy and joyous, our hearts become stayed upon the Lord in love, and the Holy Ghost will indeed become our constant companion. Does that sound impossible? I assure you, it is not. Our God is a God of miracles, and the greatest miracle is that of his love for us and trust in us.

Let's go back again to the two scriptures with which we began—those assurances that "nothing is impossible." When we have faith, nothing is impossible, because faith connects us to a source of power beyond all our ability to imagine. Because our Heavenly Father loves us, he answers our prayers in ways that build our strengths. He never exploits our weaknesses, takes advantage of our confusion, or manipulates our shortcomings. He wants us to grow, and his whole purpose is to help us grow. Our agency is eternal, and the strengths that we gain by experiencing mortality for ourselves teach us to come unto Christ and believe in him alone as our Savior. And, as Jesus reminded his disciples, fasting and prayer are great resources to increase our faith, to teach us with clarity, and to help us learn with humility.

I bear you my testimony of the Savior's love and power. I see his love manifested every day among the men and women of this Church as their love for Jesus Christ spills over into acts of service for each other. I feel the Savior's love and stand in awe and humble gratitude for his atonement. I pray that the Lord will bless us that we may use our agency to make choices wisely, that we may grow strong so that we can strengthen each other, and that we may come to Christ and exercise faith in him.

14

WALKING THROUGH THE VALLEY OF THE SHADOW

In this life, we are in the valley of the shadow. That's what mortality is. Adversity will come to all of us. But we are not alone in this valley. The Savior is with us as our companion and our shepherd. Understanding the plan of salvation is a powerful comfort and protection as we experience adversity.

The Psalmist wrote, "Yea, though I walk through the valley of the shadow of death, I will fear no evil: for thou art with me" (Psalm 23:4). While we are in mortality, we are under the shadow of death. We cannot avoid it or escape it.

I think of the immense sorrow that attends any death. I wonder at the strength and courage of our Heavenly Parents, sending us to experience mortality, and of all the deaths they have suffered through with us in our own suffering. We know something of the Father's powerful grief as he withdrew from his Son, Jesus Christ, as Christ fulfilled the Atonement and died on the cross.

One of the most terrible prayers I think any person can pray is this: "Heavenly Father, this child of mine who is suffering and in need and who is innocent before thee is also thy child. Don't you care?" And one of the reasons this prayer is so terrible is because of the answer. An endlessly loving Heavenly Father whose heart is as wide as eternity and whose attention includes perfectly and totally each child can give no answer that makes sense, that is reasonable, and that solves the problem. There is no apparent answer to some of life's pain. There is only the realization that God, our Heavenly Father, stands with us in our most anguished moments when we see the suffering of our children, that he knows what we are thinking and feeling. Though his face is hidden from us, his arms are around us.

I'd like to share with you some thoughts about my own father, a good father who died thirty-two years ago. My parents had a traditional Japanese marriage, which means that it was arranged for them by go-betweens. They did not know each other before they were married, but both of them went into that relationship trusting that their parents had picked good people who would be kind to them, who were worthy of their respect, and with whom they could build a good life. Raised in traditional homes, they both knew and understood the roles of a Japanese husband and wife. They planned to honor those commitments, and, as people of integrity, they did. They had a good and loving marriage. They were good and loving parents.

My father started to have pain in his chest in 1960 when he was fifty-eight. The doctor said there was nothing wrong, but the pain didn't go away. Even when my father went to the hospital for tests, they found nothing. Then, two years later, they discovered lung cancer that had already metastasized into his bones. So from October 1962 until February 1963 he lay in his bed at Queen's Hospital in Honolulu, as uncomplaining and patient in his dying as he had been in his living. His greatest pleasure came on the days when it was sunny and the hospital attendants would wheel his bed into a sun porch on his floor.

Ed and I were living in Colorado by then, and I was teaching school. I could not spend that time with my father; I saw him only twice during those four months. He was always very positive, and I think he tried, by pretending he would get well, to spare us any pain or any need to comfort him. "I'll come to visit you on the mainland," he would say. I respected his wish to maintain that fiction at the time, but I have wondered many times since if it would have been better to be honest, to take his hand and say, "Dad, I don't want you to die. I love you. I remember all the things you did for me and my brothers." Perhaps then he could have said things that he kept locked up in his heart, never to be spoken.

It was clear he was going to die. I knew that he was going to go, and my mother knew. The lengthy illness made her realize that he was only getting weaker and weaker. My mother was alone for much of the time with him, since my brothers were working. One of the things that helped my mother deal with this huge approaching change in her life was the kindness of the doctors and the nurses. My father was a working man—not rich, not important—but they treated him with respect and care. The members of the Church in Honolulu visited my father, a Buddhist, as well, as an act of kindness and friendship to us. Walter Teruya, who had baptized Ed, would come to visit my father and sit with him. Joyce Teruya's mother and my father's stepmother were sisters, so she came often to be with him, as cheerful and as loving to him as a daughter. I was greatly comforted, knowing that she was there in my stead. My mother's sisters and brothers also came.

When my father slipped into his final illness, my mother telephoned me, and I was able to make arrangements to join them in Hawaii. Dad was in a coma and did not respond to us, but we talked to him, sat with him, and held his hand. It seemed a hard thing to be there, wanting to tell him the love I had in my heart, wanting to tell him good-bye but feeling that he had already slipped beyond us. It was a sore place on my heart.

We were all staying at my brother's house in Honolulu—my mother, my younger brother, Tsugio, who lived in California, and I. I was sleeping on the couch. The exhaustion of the long flight and the strain of the day at the hospital, seeing my father slipping quietly away, caught up with me, and I shed many tears quietly to myself as I lay there in the stillness. I did not know when I fell asleep, but I was awakened by the feeling of something brushing quickly past my hair. The end of the couch was next to the front door, and I thought that my brother had come home from the hospital and stroked my hair as he passed. Then I heard the phone ring. When I answered it, it was the nurse from the hospital saying that Dad had passed away.

Later, we talked about this incident. My brother had been home for hours before the phone rang, and the touch on my hair that had awakened me had not come from him. In fact, my brother said, just before the phone rang he had been wakened by the sound of knocking at the window, but he thought he was dreaming.

My mother quietly said, "The Japanese say that when the spirit departs, it will return once more to the home and leave a message for the person in greatest need." Hiro had recently divorced and my father had been very worried about him. And perhaps the touch on my hair was a gentle caress, the way he used to stroke my hair when I was a little girl, to tell me that he knew I was there and that he loved me.

My mother was calm and serene, as always. She thought much and said little. There was not enough money for Ed and the boys to come, so I was there alone, a daughter in the family that had now lost its father. I felt great grief and loss on my own account, but I was more concerned about my mother. She and my father had been married for forty-one years. Being a wife and a mother was all that she had ever known. Her children had grown up and left, and now her husband was dead. What would her life be like?

The funeral was a Buddhist service in a mortuary chapel in Honolulu. Buddhist priests performed the ceremony of chanted prayers, burning incense, and softly sounded gongs. I didn't understand it, but it was very reverent and there was a feeling of peace. My mother wept quietly throughout the service and, as part of the ceremony, she, my brothers, and I came up to the casket, looked upon my father's face for the last time, and bid him farewell. My brother Hiro had fiercely insisted on a fine casket, the way his grief found expression. Then my father was cremated and his ashes were given to my mother.

A fragment of the service was Christian; as we assembled in the mortuary, the organ was playing "I Need Thee Every Hour" for the prelude. Throughout the service I kept thinking of the plan of salvation, knowing that my father was in the spirit world meeting the family.

Grief and pain come to all of us; all must endure loss as we pass through the valley of the shadow in mortality. Leslie Marmon Silko wrote, "When someone dies, you don't 'get over it' by forgetting. You 'get over it' by remembering." I have told the story of my father because I want to remember. I want us to remember what happens to us, the good and the bad.

And one of the most important things I want us to remember is that we are not alone in this valley. The Savior is with us as our companion and our shepherd. Understanding the plan of salvation is a powerful comfort and protection as we experience adversity.

When a family member or a friend slips away from the circle of those who loved him so much and counted on him for that steady affection, aching loneliness remains behind. I know what that loneliness feels like. These have been hard years, since my husband's death in 1992, but faith has made them easier for me. Each religion must help its followers deal with the great mysteries of birth and death and explain the meaning of life. When I was growing up as a little Buddhist girl, I hungered for religious truth and willingly accepted the good teachings of Buddhism about how to be an ethical and moral person. But when I encountered Mormonism, it answered in a satisfying way my hungry questions: Where did I come from? Why am I here? Where am I going?

Answers to such questions in the gospel make it easier to accept and live through our painful moments. Every human being who was ever born on the earth—you, me, all of our parents, all of our children, everyone—assembled in a great council in heaven before the creation of this earth to discuss the next step. We believe that a central core of personality, identity, and self-awareness is eternal and has always existed, but already we had experienced one major change. We had received spirit bodies by being born into the eternal family of our Heavenly Father and our Heavenly Mother as their spirit children; their firstborn in the spirit was Jesus Christ. We know that we understood more during the council in heaven than we do now. We know that we saw differently, saw with clarity how the trials of mortality were linked to a love of the Savior and of our Heavenly Father.

At that council in heaven, we saw the Father's plan for us— that we could leave his presence and come to an earth that he would create for us, where we would gain physical bodies like his and learn to walk by faith and use our agency to choose good, life, and love or evil, darkness, and death. We "shouted for joy," the scriptures say, because we could see that this was the great plan of happiness.

There was opposition. Another spirit son of God, called Lucifer or Satan, wanted to deprive us of our agency. In return he guaranteed that we would all return. We thus had to make a choice: Would we choose freedom with its possibility that we might become evil but also its promise that we might become like God, or would we abandon our agency and never learn faith, love, and obedience?

We knew we would make mistakes, be subject to the limitations of mortality, and suffer—but Jesus Christ promised that he would be our Savior. He would be born to a mortal mother, enter this world to teach us how to return to our Heavenly Parents, and, through the sacrifice of the Atonement, redeem us from our sins. We had no question that he would keep his promise, and we bound ourselves by covenant to accept him as our Savior.

We are here, in these mortal bodies, because we chose the Father's plan. This fact should be a source of great hope and confidence to us. We all trusted the Father. We all loved the Savior. We all chose their plan once. This should give us confidence that we can continue to seek the Savior's way, recognize his voice, and make correct choices.

But of course, being here in mortality also means that none of us is perfect and we do not live in a perfect world. We all make mistakes. We all suffer. We all need to repent. We all desperately need the Savior—to teach us how to live and how to love, to teach us faith, and to teach us to choose obedience freely, not because we are compelled.

And so, the earth was created. Adam and Eve were placed in the garden of Eden, made the choices that separated them from the daily, visible presence of God, and began the human cycle of birth, work, suffering and joy, doubt and faith, choice, experience, understanding, acceptance of the Savior's atonement, and eventual physical death. This is a cycle that all of us enter. We will all go through it. And when we die, we will go first to a place of spirits where we will associate with one another, knowing each other there as we know each other here, but more clearly because we will be freed from mortal limitations. Then comes the judgment, and then the resurrection when we will again be in our Heavenly Father's presence. But that is not the end of our progression, for progression is eternal. Some of us will have learned the lessons of mortality well and used our time here to become like Heavenly Father. Others will still have much to learn, partly because of limitations over which they had no control during their earthly experiences and partly because of how they used their agency.

I find great hope in this plan of salvation. Regardless of our limitations and achievements in this life, all of us will have many opportunities to continue to grow, even in the next life. Our Heavenly Father does not give up on any of his children, any more than we give up on our own children.

Jesus Christ, though he was without sin, entered the same cycle, participated in the same experiences. In Gethsemane he endured every pang of guilt, every sorrow at loss, every form of suffering that we know. He was with my Buddhist father as he patiently endured the increasing pain of cancer. He was with my mother as she wept quietly by the open coffin. We do not walk through the valley of the shadow alone.

The Book of Mormon tells us: "This life [is] a probationary state; a time to prepare to meet God; a time to prepare for that endless state which has been spoken of by us, which is after the resurrection of the dead" (Alma 12:24).

O how great [is] the plan of our God! For on the other hand, the paradise of God must deliver up the spirits of the righteous, and the grave deliver up the body of the righteous; and the spirit and the body is restored to itself again, and all [people] become incorruptible, and immortal, and they are living souls, having a perfect knowledge like unto us in the flesh, save it be that our knowledge shall be perfect.

Wherefore, we shall have a perfect knowledge of all our guilt, and our uncleanness, and our nakedness; and the righteous shall have a perfect knowledge of their enjoyment, and their righteousness, being clothed with purity, yea, even with the robe of righteousness. (2 Nephi 9:13–14)

Jesus Christ redeems all of us from temporal death because of his own resurrection. And if we choose to follow his teachings, we are redeemed from spiritual death, or a separation from God, as well. We can be with God in kingdoms of glory in the next life.

We know that Jesus is our advocate with the Father. John reminded the Saints of his day: "If any [one] sin, we have an advocate with the Father, Jesus Christ the righteous" (1 John 2:1). Half a dozen times, Jesus Christ told Joseph Smith and the early Saints: "Lift up your hearts and be glad, for I am in your midst, and am your advocate with the Father; and it is his good will to give you the kingdom" (D&C 29:5; see also D&C 32:3; 62:1; 110:4).

Because the Savior came and fulfilled his mission, we can bid farewell to a departed loved one knowing that the separation is only for a short time, that he or she has gone to paradise, where the spirits of the righteous await the resurrection, when our bodies will be restored to us, perfected and in glory. And if a person's life was filled with challenges and mistakes, we can have confidence that he or she will be in a place of learning and knowledge where people can continue to grow and progress.

I have faith that Ed is in paradise. I think of the friends and loved ones who have made the transition from mortality. I can almost see Ed's face, beaming with joy, as he reaches out to take their hands in a loving welcome.

I have felt Ed's concern and presence many times over the years since his death. I know that he still loves me, our sons, and the rest of his family. I also know that part of what we came to earth to learn is how to walk in faith, even at times of great sorrow. When sorrow comes to you, it will test your faith but will also build your faith if you turn to the Savior.

Losing Ed was the hardest thing in my life. I accepted Ed's death, my faith was strong, and I had the love and support of my sons, our family, and many, many friends—but I was still bewildered and disoriented by grief. I groped for the hand of the Savior. I went back again and again in prayer, asking for strength for each new day, asking for comfort, asking for patience, asking for the ability to serve others rather than be absorbed by my own sorrow. Each of those prayers was answered in the measure I needed. I could feel myself becoming stronger every day. I could feel my ability to endure in patience growing. When my moments of sorrow and loneliness and weeping came, I could accept them. A great source of strength was the knowledge that kept ringing in my heart, "I don't have to do this by myself." You don't have to do it by yourself either. "When ye shall search for me with all your heart," the Lord told Jeremiah, "ye shall . . . find me" (Jeremiah 29:13). "Trust in me," says the Savior. "A hair of [your] head shall not fall to the ground unnoticed" (D&C 84:116). "The very hairs of your head are all numbered. Fear not therefore: ye are of more value than many sparrows" (Luke 12:7).

When we lose a righteous person who is dear to us, we have the wonderful opportunity to honor that person by incorporating the best principles from his or her life into ours. What were his gifts? What were her talents? A desire to serve, a happy outlook on life, generosity with material possessions, an even greater generosity in having a heart that included everyone? Following the example of a loved one, we can love the Lord, make covenants with the Lord, and keep them faithfully. We too can seek to understand the Savior's great mission of atonement, redemption, and salvation. We too can seek to become worthy followers of the Son of God. And we too can anticipate that when the time comes for us to step through the veil of mortality, leaving our failing and pain-filled bodies behind, we will see the loving smile and feel the welcoming embrace, not only of our Heavenly Parents and of the Savior, but also of our loved ones who will greet us in full vigor, full remembrance, and full love.

When we are in the valley of the shadow, it is a time of questions without answers. We ask, "How can I bear this? Why did such a good woman have to die? Why aren't my prayers being answered?" In this life, we will not receive answers to many questions of "why"—partly because the limitations of mortality prevent us from understanding the full plan.

But I testify to you that the answer of faith is a powerful one, even in the most difficult of circumstances, because it does not depend on us—on our strength to endure, on our willpower, on the depth of our intellectual understanding, or on the resources we can accumulate. No, it depends on God, whose strength is omnipotence, whose understanding is that of eternity, and who has the will to walk beside us in love, sharing our burden.

He could part the Red Sea before us or calm the angry storm that besets us, but these would be small miracles for the God of nature. Instead, he chooses to do something harder: He wants to transform human nature into divine nature. And thus, when our Red Sea blocks our way and when the storm threatens to overwhelm us, he enters the water with us, holding us in the hands of love, supporting us with the arms of mercy. When we emerge from the valley of the shadow, we will see that he was there with us all the time.

15

HUBS AND SPOKES: SOME THOUGHTS ON WHEELS

Think for a moment about the role wheels play in our lives. They keep our machines going. They're a symbol of forward progress. We talk about "not reinventing the wheel" when we mean that we should build on the work that has already been done. We talk about the turn of fortune's wheel that raises some to high position and then, almost as if it were a natural law, lets them fall again to the dust. We talk about "wheels within wheels" when we mean that a situation is politically or emotionally complicated. We salute our leaders as "big wheels." We sing about putting our shoulders to the wheel.

You know what a classic wheel looks like: the hub at the center to provide a place for the axle and for the spokes simultaneously, the spokes radiating outward at even intervals to the rim, and the rim making a larger circle than the hub but one that is exactly parallel to it. I want you to meditate, for a moment, on the fact that a wheel would not be round if it did not contain some shapes that are the antithesis of round. Visualize what would happen if we took the spokes out of the wheel. Right, CUH-RUNCH! and that would be the end of forward motion.

And now visualize what would happen if we took the rim off the wheel so that these spokes were just sticking out into space. With the first turn of the wheel, the first pressure on these spokes would rip them from their sockets and we'd hear that ominous crunching sound again that would bring our forward motion to a sudden halt.

Well, if we can't remove the rim and we can't remove the spokes, what would happen if we removed the hub? Again, with the first attempt to move forward, with the slightest pressure, the wheel would collapse again.

So all three parts are essential: hub, spoke, and rim. If we say that the wheel in its entirety represents our ward, then I want to compare the hub to our testimony of Jesus Christ. It's the smallest part of the wheel, the one that takes up the least space, but the entire wheel is organized around it. As members, let's say that we're the spokes, lots of us, each with our own space, our own connections to the hub and to the rim. And the rim is where we come in contact with the world. It's our daily lives. Some of the roads we roll over are pretty dusty. Some of them are pretty rocky. And as spokes, we often have a very limited view of the whole. We know the spokes that are nearest to us, but sometimes we misunderstand those that are across the wheel from us.

For instance, let's say that we have a spoke that ends in the rim of the wheel that is at the very top of its revolution—right up on top. It can see the road ahead and behind. It can look out across the green fields. It can feel the sunshine and hear the birds. Then it looks down and sees, directly across from it, another spoke that is embedded in the part of the rim that touches the road. It's buried in dust. It can't see a thing. It can't hear anything but the gritting of the dirt particles against each other. No sunshine, no birds for it.

What if the spoke on top judged the spoke on the bottom? What if Sunny Spoke said, even in her heart, "Well, look at old Dusty. No culture, no advantages, no appreciation of the finer things available. Why doesn't she get her head out of the mud and rise to the finer things of life?"

159

None of us knows where the revolutions of this wheel of fortune will take us, whether we'll have sunshine or adversity. None of us can judge anyone else. We simply don't know what another's circumstances are, and we don't know what's in someone else's heart.

Elder James Paramore gave one of the most loving explanations of our Christian responsibilities for each other that I've ever heard: "No Christian should ever be a challenge to another Christian. . . . When we seek to follow Christ, we take the oath of a Christian as a member of this church; we covenant to never put another in any sort of prison, but rather try to liberate those who are there."[1]

It's easier to refrain from judging others if we concentrate on the hub instead of on the rim. We're all in this church because we have testimonies of Jesus Christ. We're here because we have all taken his name upon us, felt the power of the redemption in our lives, and felt within us the stirrings and whisperings of the Spirit. Sometimes we might think, "Well, So-and-so is no advertisement for the Church." Don't say it. Don't even think it. We just don't know what miracles of grace might have already worked in that person's heart, how much difference there is already between him and the man he might have been without the gospel. None of us understand the gospel in the same way, live it the same way, or live it perfectly.

Think of the wheel again. Out on the rim, the spokes are far apart. Each one has a long space between it and its neighbor. But at the hub, the spokes are close together. They almost touch. Our shared testimonies and faith bring us close together even when our life circumstances may separate us by wide distances. Circumstances can change drastically. They can change because of forces over which we have no control or because of decisions that we make and carry out.

Certainly a growing testimony of the gospel means that there will be constant changes in how we live our lives. Elder Paramore spoke about a convert who said that joining the Church "changed the way he thought, the way he talked, the way he believed, the way he dressed, the way he worked and honored his employer, the things he read, the movies he saw, the way he conducted his financial affairs in absolute honesty with everyone, and the way he served others." These were all life-style choices he made to bring his life more into harmony with the teachings of the Savior. But even more important are the subtle miracles that the power of the Atonement works in our lives when we begin to walk by faith. As Elder Paramore says, "Beloved friends, it is Jesus who has unlocked and will unlock the doors of our personal prisons. It is a glorious promise to all who are captive, for whatever reasons, upon the condition of repentance."[2]

I don't want us merely to stop judging other people because they're different from us. I want us to enjoy each other's diversity, appreciate all the different styles we have of being individually righteous, and learn from that diversity. After all, what if you went out to your garden every day from March until October and it just had beans in it? Even if you adored beans, wouldn't you like a little variety? Friends in my ward have been so generous about sharing fresh lettuce, peas, corn, zucchini, and tomatoes with me. Even though I don't have a garden of my own, I've enjoyed the diversity and variety of theirs. And our own differences mean that I'm grateful when someone comes with zucchini instead of responding, "Oh, no, not more zucchini! I have two hundred in the backyard!"

On second thought, though, I *do* have a garden. It's a garden that one of my friends planted on our faculty bulletin board at Sunrise Elementary, where I was principal. It includes some vegetables we could all use:

First plant five rows of peas: patience, promptness, preparation, perseverance, and purity. Next plant three rows of squash: squash gossip, squash criticism, squash indifference. Then plant five rows of lettuce: Let-us be faithful to duty, let-us be unselfish, let-us be loyal, let-us be true to obligation, and let-us love one another. And no garden is complete without turnips: Turn-up for important meetings, turn-up with a smile, turn-up with good ideas, turn-up with determination to make everything good and worthwhile.[3]

Now, if it's not too confusing to have wheels going through our vegetable garden, can we remember that the hub is Christ. By staying close to Christ, we can be close to each other, even when the circumstances of our daily lives mean that we find ourselves in very different places. We need to allow for differences, appreciate them, and enjoy them in each other.

Keeping Wheels in Motion

Another thing about wheels that I want to discuss is a particular characteristic of bicycles: the wheel has to keep moving or it will wobble and fall over sideways. To me, this means that we have to keep trying, keep working, keep doing our best, even if we'd just like to stop sometimes.

When we were living in Colorado and the boys were about ages twelve and thirteen, we decided that a wonderful family activity would be to ride bikes together. There was just one problem. I'd never ridden a bike in my life, and I just couldn't make my mind work fast enough or hard enough to imagine how a bicycle with only two wheels could stay up.

But the boys insisted I could do it, and I thought I should at least try. We lived on a quiet street, so after dinner, we'd all go out with my bicycle. Ed would stay with me at the corner, and the boys would station themselves at intervals down the block. I'd climb on—oh, no! it was wobbling already!—and Ed would give me a push and yell, "Pedal!" And I'd pedal and wobble and lose control and tip over before I got to the first boy.

We did that for a whole week. I had bruised knees and a bruised ego. The boys got very bored waiting down the block for me to get even that far. "Gee, Mom," they admitted, "you embarrass us." We tried children's size bikes. We tried a girl's banana bike. Nothing worked. I just kept tipping over. Ken suggested, semi-seriously, that we put training wheels on my bike. But it was Ed who found the perfect solution. He bought a tandem bike, and I was just as happy as could be, pedaling along with Ed while the boys swooped around us on their bikes.

I think the problem was that I kept thinking about falling over instead of about pedaling—and so, of course, I fell over. Sometimes the same problem afflicts us as we try to keep our own wheels in motion. It takes a lot of work. It looks scary ahead of us. And we can visualize failure all too easily. I'd like to suggest that we keep pedaling.

As Latter-day Saints, we know that our work and our service are not merely to fill a few hours or a few years while we are on this earth. They have eternal consequences and the potential to bring us happiness and great glory. President Spencer W. Kimball tried to give an audience of young adults at the Salt Lake Institute of Religion a glimpse of their eternal potential with these words that are also, I think, applicable to us in whatever stage of life we happen to be in:

> Each one of you has it within the realm of his possibility to develop a kingdom over which you will preside as its king and god. You will need to develop yourself and grow in ability and power and worthiness, to govern such a world with all of its people. You are sent to this earth not merely to have a good time or to satisfy urges or passions or desires. You are sent to this earth, not to ride merry-go-rounds, airplanes, automobiles, and have what the world calls "fun." You are sent to school, for that matter, to begin as a human infant, and grow to unbelievable proportions in wisdom, judgment, knowledge and power. . . . That is why in our childhood and in our young adulthood we must stretch and grow and remember and prepare for the later life when limitations will terminate so that we can go on and on and on.[4]

I'm about four decades in age beyond where most of the students were that President Kimball was speaking to, but I still think that this applies to me. Maybe you, too? Let's keep pedaling. You know that when you have a certain amount of momentum, you can sail right over bumps; if you're going too slowly, they can make you lose your grip on the handlebars.

I was inspired to learn the story of June Leifson, the former dean of BYU's College of Nursing. She's a hero who overcame many bumps in her personal road and triumphed because she just kept pedaling. She was born with a double cleft palate, which made it difficult for her to speak intelligibly and caused significant disfigurement of her face. The doctors did not expect her to live, but her parents fed her from an eyedropper, taught five brothers and four sisters to love and support her, and steadfastly sustained her through the agonizing series of operations required to correct the palate and the tissue grafts to rebuild her mouth and nose.

Even her family questioned whether she would be able to handle the challenges of college. "[My father] did not want to risk my being hurt," she said, "but he had instilled in us a deep love of learning, and I knew I had to earn my baccalaureate. Once he knew I was determined to get a university education, he was extremely supportive."

She had dreamed since childhood of being a nurse, following in the footsteps of a pediatric nurse at LDS Hospital where June received most of her surgeries. This woman always "made me feel loved and protected. . . . There was never any doubt that I wanted to become a nurse just like the best of them." But her application was rejected, and one administrator told her "she should never consider nursing because she would frighten the patients, and they would not be able to understand her." Crushed by the rejections and traumatized by her own inability to speak, she determinedly persevered, underwent five additional operations during her first two years of college, and engaged in "intense speech therapy."

She was finally admitted to BYU on probation, earned a bachelor's degree, nursed for many years, and then returned to college to earn a master's degree and a Ph.D. In 1986, she was named dean of the BYU College of Nursing.[5]

You too have dreams, goals, and aspirations. Some of them may be on about the same order as my decision to ride a bicycle. You may have abandoned some dreams because you have thought, "There's no way I can achieve it. It's too hard. The road is too bumpy. I'll fall over. I'll embarrass myself or my children." Don't be too quick to make that decision. I've done many things in my life that are much more difficult than learning to ride a bicycle, but in that case I let my vivid imagination stop me when I could have let it work for me. But be creative and ingenious, too. Maybe there's a tandem-bicycle possibility in the two-wheeled project you have in mind, and maybe you don't have to do it all by yourself.

Whatever you decide, don't give up. Let your hard work count for something. After all, Latter-day Saints are experts on making miracles happen. Keep pedaling!

Big Wheels, Little Wheels

Wheels come in all sizes—some are big and some are little. It's normal for us to be impressed by size, to think that bigger is better. Once when I was driving along a highway, the traffic was stopped for some construction equipment and I was right next to a gigantic earthmover for a few minutes. Now, I drive an Explorer, so it's pretty high off the ground. I'm used to looking over traffic instead of seeing people's trunks. When I looked out my window and saw a wheel that topped my roof by two or three feet, I thought, "Now *there's* a big wheel!"

In the Church, because of the efficiency of our organization, it's nearly always clear who's in charge, who has the responsibility for a function, or who is presiding at a meeting. Even though Jesus made it clear that his definition of "the greatest" is the person who is the "servant of all," we sometimes fall into worldly ways of thinking, even in the Church. I call this the "big wheel" syndrome.

We think, because we're in charge, that we're important, and we expect other people to treat us as if we were important.

I received some insights about this concept when I was conducting an information-gathering session with some Relief Society presidents in an inner-city area on the East Coast. Gladys Newkirk, a very candid black woman, said that she was concerned about self-sufficient presidencies who put themselves on pedestals and who obviously saw themselves as the big wheels. Gladys hastened to add that she *knew* these women were not doing this on purpose, but the results were still damaging to the feeling of sisterhood. She recalls her hurt when someone made a racial remark to her face. But even that hurt her less than coming to a social and offering to help, only to have the woman she asked, someone who was in the president's little clique, just look at her and shrug. Gladys described how pained she was to look around the Relief Society room, to see sisters shrinking under the burden of feeling that they did not belong, and then to see that the Relief Society presidency was apparently oblivious to it.

What I liked about Gladys was her realism. She knew that this inequality was wrong, but she accepted that some of it was probably inevitable. Rather than rage on about it, she suggested a way to use it to increase sisterhood. She pointed out the social reality that a person's position gives her a lot of "clout," and that when an important person like the Relief Society president notices you and talks with you, it makes you feel "ten feet tall."

Gladys, now a Relief Society president herself, then gave an eloquent plea for more sensitivity:

> I know that the worth of a soul is equal in God's sight. I feel that it is up to each person in that Relief Society presidency . . . and any other person who holds an "upper calling," if you will, to zoom in, and pick out someone who is not as aggressive, someone who may be introverted, someone who may be shy, someone who may need some special help. Don't just sit back and look at that person go further and further down. Do

166

something about it. I think it is our responsibility—and not only the presidency but particularly the presidency, for each one to grab hold of someone . . . and don't let them go.[6]

I suspect that the problem of belonging exists whenever there are transition points, in-groups and out-groups, move-ins, converts, or social and economic disparities of any kind. You know, to a new and insecure sister or brother, even a little thing like volunteering to read a scripture in class can take an enormous amount of courage.

Don't we all want to go home to our Heavenly Father and bring those we love with us? Don't we all want to be spiritually alive in Christ instead of suffering the spiritual death of separation from his spirit? And don't we want the comfort of closeness in our families and our wards? Big wheels and little wheels are all rolling toward the same destination.

If we were to look at your position on a ward organizational chart, perhaps we would perceive you as a "big wheel." Or maybe you feel very much like a little wheel. Remember that the measure of service is not who does it but whether it's done with love and happiness.

Are we happy in our service to others? Do we find joy in ministering to others, or are we more comfortable when we are engaged in administrative routines and duties, dealing with other administrators? If the prophet were here, would we not rush to serve him in any way we could? But big wheels who serve only other big wheels are forgetting that Jesus, the head of this Church, said that when we served "the least of these" we were performing the same act for him. That helps keep things in perspective, doesn't it?

The next time you climb in your car, or swing your leg over your bicycle, or strap on a pair of roller blades, I want you to think, just for a moment, about wheels. Remember that the hub is Christ, and as long as we concentrate on our shared faith in Christ, we will be close together, even if our places on the rim are widely separated, sometimes in the mud or dust, and sometimes in the sunshine. We don't need to judge others for their circumstances. We can accept each other's diversity and rejoice in it.

Second, remember the point about work. Don't let your bicycle tip over because you concentrate on the bumps and on visualizing, in exquisite detail, how you're going to crash to the sidewalk. Work hard. Do your best. And let your work count for something.

And the third point is about big wheels and little wheels. Being called as a leader, or having influence or special knowledge or even the comfortableness of knowing that you belong firmly to your Relief Society, does not give you special privileges. Instead it gives you special responsibilities to reach out to others who don't feel equally comfortable. Strengthen them, and let them strengthen you. In so doing, we will follow the way of the Savior, who urged the Nephites: "Therefore, hold up your light that it may shine unto the world. Behold I am the light which ye shall hold up" (3 Nephi 18:24).

16

LIVES WOVEN TOGETHER

There's more than one right way to be a Mormon woman, just as there's more than one right way to be a quilt. We don't always control our days or the shapes of our lives. There are days that are square with neatly turned corners and days when only creative feather-stitching keeps us anchored to the pieces next to us. And some days are a lot crazier than others!

I want to discuss the stitching that keeps us together. I think that stitching is our sisterhood in the gospel. I want to encourage us to make each contact we have with another woman one of kindness and respect, because we never know what kinds of connections we are weaving. Sometimes we're afraid of someone who seems different. Sometimes we feel desperately duty-bound to defend our own life choices, to the extent that we have to think women who have made other choices are wrong. A great burden is lifted from my heart every time I think of the scripture, "Judge not, that ye be not judged" (Matthew 7:1). I don't want to judge. I want to accept, to understand, to love, and to help where I can.

Take just one area where women can be dreadfully hard on themselves and on other women. That's motherhood. I thought of this when I was thumbing through a collection of schoolchildren's observations about mothers. Do any of these sound familiar?

Libby complains, "Mothers say no, no before the child can ever tell her what she wants but I think mothers should let them finnish." Sigh. We all know that feeling, don't we?

Lizann thinks, "She knows what is important. That is why God asked them to be a mother." Don't we wish?

Laura says, "A mother is just like God except God is better." Right. *Lots* better.

Joe sounds a little resentful, "A mother spanks you, but only for a reason, and that reason your supposed to know."

Harry thinks mothers make miracles: "If I forget to tell my mother I need my sheperd costume tomorrow morning, she finds one in the night. That is a mother!"

Gary whines, "A mother doesn't do anything except she wants to. Nobody makes her take baths and naps or takes away her frog."

And then this realistic comment from Elliott: "Mothers always shout pick up your things and they mostly end up doing it themself."[1]

I think that mothers by and large do the very best they know how to do, even if they get blindsided by circumstances, by immaturity, by bad habits, and by their own lack of vision. I love the experience that Annette Paxman Bowen reported about her own up-and-down feelings about motherhood. She wrote:

> On Mother's Day, my husband, then a Navy flight surgeon, had to spend the day at the hospital. As I hurried and scurried about the house getting our two boys, who were just four and two, ready for church, I somehow offended my oldest son. He scowled and muttered, "I hate mothers!" Undaunted, I scooted the boys out the door, and once they were safely belted in their seats, I told my son that he needed to think of three nice things to say about me; after all, it was Mother's Day. He screwed up his face and thought about it for a mile or two, then announced, "Gosh, Mom, I can think of two things, but *three* is real hard!"

Sister Bowen commented ruefully, "I learned that day that my self-esteem could not be dependent on my children." Then she went on to talk about an experience that really *did* boost her self-esteem:

> One of the most refreshing experiences of this year was the night, while setting tables and cooking food for a Relief Society dinner, when five women and I confessed how we *really* ran our homes. The truth came out: we often cooked in a hurry and didn't fix elaborate meals; we told of our personal home-management foibles, disasters, and child-rearing woes; and (this was the real moment of truth) we confessed how often we changed the sheets on our beds. We laughed so heartily that a man walked over from the other side of the building and said, "I'm sorry to interrupt, but I really have to see what's going on. I'm sure I'm missing something wonderful." And he was. I went home from the church that night feeling reassured. I was not inadequate. I was not a failure. I felt blissfully *normal.*[2]

Isn't that a great gift we can give each other—being honest about our own lives and withholding judgment about someone else's life? My daughter-in-law's mother sent me a fascinating clipping about Heloise, as in "Hints from Heloise." The original Heloise had been the current Heloise's mother. She had started writing a column for the *Honolulu Advertiser* in 1959 when she realized that the household hints she was swapping with the other young military wives, far from their mothers, probably could reach a wider audience. When she died suddenly of a heart attack, her daughter was twenty years old and had been working with her mother for a few years. She had only twenty-four hours to decide whether she would continue the column or not.

Put yourself in this young woman's place. If your mother had created a public persona known to thousands, some of whom appreciated it and some of whom made fun of it, would you want to step into those shoes, especially if you were only twenty?

Wouldn't you have thought, "Does this mean that I'll become my mother? Will I ever have a life of my own? Who will I be, really?" I think it says a great deal for both mother and daughter that the current Heloise took up her mother's name and her mother's work and, after twenty years, says with great satisfaction, "I can't imagine doing anything else!"

And do you know what distillation of wisdom Heloise has for the women of the world? She says: "Maybe life's not perfect, but was life perfect for people living through the Great Depression, through W[orld] W[ar] II, and so forth? I think we all need to lighten up—on ourselves, on others. So what if the Thanksgiving pie didn't turn out. Will you remember the bad pie in 20 years[?] No, you'll remember being with your family. In this complex and difficult world, the basic truths always have, and still do apply."[3]

So take it from Heloise and take it from me—each contact that we make with another woman in our lives is weaving a connection. Make it a strong connection, a warm connection, a kind and respectful connection. Be honest about your own life and your own feelings. Accept without judging the life and circumstances of your sisters.

Think about your own ward and the women in it. Let me compare our wards to a satellite picture of a whole continent. As we scan over it, we have a lot of variety. There's a jungle here, a mountain range here, a lake over there, and a desert on the other side of it. Each of these systems is connected, of course, but each is also separate. Then a boundary is drawn around a certain part of this landscape, and we have a corner of the lake, a bit of jungle, three of the lower foothills, and quite a lot of desert all encircled within the same boundary. All of these ecological systems are told that they are important to each other, that they need to understand each other, that they need to get along with each other.

Think about it for a moment. A ward is based on two minimal requirements: we live within the same geographical boundary and we've been baptized with the same baptism. When we pick friends, we may have a whole assortment of things in common—the same educational background, children of the same ages, husbands who went to high school together, a fondness for fudge, or a passion for tennis. Well, Heavenly Father doesn't say that those things are wrong or bad, but when it comes to dealing with other members of the Church, he tells us that people don't have to meet complex or exacting criteria to be worthy of our esteem and our love.

I've always thought it interesting that the apostle Paul reminds the Galatian Saints: "As we have therefore opportunity, let us do good unto all [people], especially unto them who are of the household of faith" (Galatians 6:10). Why do you think he says, "*especially* unto them who are of the household of faith"? It sounds almost as if he expected it to be harder to do good to members than to nonmembers, as if it would take an extra measure of charity and compassion to deal lovingly with those who are members. I believe that this is often so.

With the Ephesians, Paul pled:

I . . . beseech you that ye walk worthy of the vocation wherewith ye are called,

With all lowliness and meekness, with longsuffering, forbearing one another in love;

Endeavouring to keep the unity of the Spirit in the bond of peace.

There is one body, and one Spirit, even as ye are called in one hope of your calling;

One Lord, one faith, one baptism,

One God and Father of all, who is above all, and through all, and in you all.

But unto every one of us is given grace according to the measure of the gift of Christ. (Ephesians 4:1–7)

He was reminding the Ephesian Saints, just as we need to remind ourselves, that the strength to be good members of our wards and to have steadfast love in our hearts for our sisters does

173

not really depend on our willpower but on the Lord's grace. We can do it, not because we're good but because he's good.

Is that really enough? Can you really feel sisterhood for women when the only things you have in common are where you live and your baptism? You know, I think you can. And the reason I think it is because, if you move forward in faith with the love of God in your heart to reach out to a sister, the love of God will spill over into love of that sister, and you will discover that you have many things in common.

Let me tell you a story about a sister with whom you probably have very, very little in common, who responded to our request to send us an experience about how Relief Society had helped her. Fumiko Otake, a sister from Yamagata, Japan, had a husband who was not a member of the Church. He very often traveled on business, so she managed to attend church almost every other week. She was deeply impressed by a Relief Society lesson that told the sisters it would make their homes more pleasant if they would say "Good morning" to their husbands. In forty years of marriage, she had never greeted him in this way—it seemed too direct, too personal—although she would say other things like "Birds are singing this morning" or "It's a nice day today." When she finally worked up her nerve to say "Good morning," he was flabbergasted, but obviously he thought about it all day, because the next day, he greeted *her* with "Good morning." It brought a new dimension into their relationship, and they had a very loving and intimate bond for the last three years of his life, before he died unexpectedly. "I can't thank the Relief Society enough for its teachings," Sister Otake wrote.[4]

Now, you may be feeling a little puzzled about why the saying of "Good morning" seemed such an immense hurdle to overcome and how such a simple greeting could make such a difference in Sister Otake's marriage. I chose the story on purpose because it *is* a little mysterious. There's something about the culture that leaves us perplexed and confused. But we don't have to understand the mystery about "Good morning" to recognize two other facts about Sister Otake that probably resonate within our own hearts: She wanted to have a better relationship with her husband, and she had the faith to try a suggestion that came to her through the Relief Society lessons. I think that we can all relate to those two principles in Sister Otake's life. The great sisterhood of Relief Society transcends many boundaries of the world.

We are used to thinking of ourselves as daughters of our Heavenly Father and as children of Christ, but have you stopped to think that we are also the sisters of Christ by virtue of our descent from the same Heavenly Parents? We stood beside Christ valiantly in the premortal existence when it was time to choose whether we would risk mortality by faith, with its possibility of failure and its certainty of pain but also its promise of growth and glory. We accepted the grace of Christ in trust and hope. We felt his love for us and responded with our own love. Does that give you a feeling for the remarkable power that we possess as a result of our premortal heritage? We have the ability to recognize the truth. We have the power to reach out in faith and love to others. We have the strength to endure to the end of this life, no matter what our trials, because we have already accepted Christ as our Savior, once when we stood in his presence and again when we entered the waters of baptism.

What does it mean to bear the name of Christ? Let me suggest perhaps a different way to think about that concept than we may usually have. One of the interesting items in the article about Heloise is her real name: Ponce Kiah Marchelle Heloise Cruse Evans. Now *that's* a name! Think about your own name for a minute. Is it a name that has a meaning in another language or another culture? "Helen," for instance, means "light." My own name, "Chieko," means "child who embraces knowledge." Names are part of ourselves. We're comfortable with them. It's hard to think of ourselves as separate from our names.

We bear the name of Christ. His name is a name of power, a name of promise, a name of performance. If the name of Christ is in our hearts, if we experience the change of heart that comes when we make place for that name, then we have the power that we would expect from a sister of Christ in doing good and bringing about the redemption of God's children.

The Psalmist captures for me the same idea in his words, "When thou saidst, Seek ye my face; my heart said unto thee, Thy face, Lord, will I seek" (Psalm 27:8). That's the spirit we need in our own hearts—a spirit of seeking, sensitively and thoughtfully, so that when we're trying to sort out the correct behavior or determine the right words to speak, we don't need to consult a lot of rules or struggle intellectually through balancing one principle against another. We can simply refer to our own hearts where we carry the Savior's name and his image and let his Spirit speak peace to our own hearts.

We are women of covenant. We are partners with God in the glorious work of bringing to pass the immortality and eternal lives of ourselves, of those we love, and of those whose lives we barely know we have touched.

I pray that the Spirit of the Lord will rest upon us in mighty power, that we will unite our faith in sisterhood and stand united with our priesthood brethren in the great work of redemption. May we feel the spirit of the Savior and the spirit of salvation resting upon us, that we may increase in love and faith and good works.

SIX PLEASURES OF LEADERSHIP

I don't know what your definition of leadership is, but I like this definition from E. M. Estes, former president of General Motors: "Leadership is the courage to admit mistakes, the vision to welcome change, the enthusiasm to motivate others, and the confidence to stay out of step when everyone else is marching to the wrong tune."[1]

You probably have your own definitions of leadership, based on your experiences with leaders you admire, with situations that have challenged you to provide either leadership or followership, and with the exciting ideas that you are learning for this stage of life. I want to share a personal list of leadership qualities that I think are important. First, leadership means working with people, so enjoy the processes of interaction. Second, be enthusiastic. Third, be appreciative. Fourth, be open to change. Seek it out and enjoy it. Fifth, be *kigatsuku*. Don't wait for service to find you. Seek it out. Sixth, build safe environments where self-esteem can thrive.

Enjoy the Process

I put enjoying people right at the top of my leadership list because I think it's the most important quality of leadership. Enjoy people! Enjoy what's going on!

Sometimes "leadership" seems like this enormous abstraction, sort of heroic and noble and stern. Well, even heroes have to get off their white horses and eat lunch, so my philosophy is not to get up on the white horse in the first place. White horses are frequently high horses, and somebody on a high horse is difficult to follow.

Enjoy the process. There were times when Jesus sat on a mountainside and addressed crowds of five thousand, but he was a teacher no matter where he was. When he walked through a grain field, he talked with his disciples about the process of sowing. When he was sitting in the house of Simon the leper and a woman interrupted his important conversation to pour ointment from an alabaster bottle onto his feet, he didn't consider it an interruption or an embarrassment. When he encountered a funeral procession passing through the gates of the city of Nain, he immediately responded to the terrible need of that grief-stricken mother and raised her son from the dead.

Do you understand what I'm saying about the process? Leadership has to straddle some big gaps sometimes. A leader needs to have a vision of the whole organization and the overall direction in which it is going. A leader must keep that vision clear and shining even during those times when it's slowly coming into focus and difficult to explain to someone else. But the vision of leadership isn't something that you go up on the mountain to get and come down carrying like a stone tablet. It's something you create in the little details of how you live your life every day because of the strength of your principles.

I'm convinced that Jesus' purpose in being born, fulfilling his ministry, and dying was to communicate in every interaction, in every deed, in every way, in every day two simple principles: He loves us. And we should love each other. All his behavior can be explained by going back to those principles. Consider what was probably the harshest action he took—cleansing the temple. I believe he chased the moneychangers out of the temple not because he was against commerce or because he hated moneychangers per se, but rather because they were focused on something other than loving God and were putting obstacles in the way of people who wanted to worship God. That's exactly why I think he chastised the scribes and Pharisees in such stinging terms. They were hypocrites because they claimed to love God when what they really loved was power, and they were barring access to God to the people who weren't as learned or who didn't follow the complicated rules as well as they did.

Now, those are negative experiences, but think of the dozens of positive ways in which Jesus exercised leadership—his encouragement to Peter to walk to him on the sea, stilling the storm to calm the fears of his apostles, taking the five loaves and two fishes of a young boy and feeding a multitude with them, spitting into the dirt and rubbing it on the eyelids of a man born blind so that he could see again.

Jesus enjoyed the process of leadership, all its tiny, ordinary, unspectacular interactions. He didn't sit in a cave in a mountain, or have a private office in the penthouse of some Jerusalem skyscraper. He was with the people—looking into many eyes, hearing many voices, and responding in a personal way to dozens of people every day. I think he *loved* that.

So, if you find yourself getting all pompous and stuffy and noble and heroic because, after all, you are "A Leader," or if you are developing a martyr complex because of all the crushing burdens you bear, lighten up! Leadership is a blessing and a joy, so enjoy it. Enjoy the people, and enjoy the process.

Be Enthusiastic

The second quality on my personal leadership list is a natural outgrowth of the first one. If you're enjoying the people and enjoying the process, then you'll probably already feel enthusiastic.

Are you reading this book indoors? If so, chances are you are able to see the pages clearly because of a lamp or fixture with electric light bulbs. We owe these light bulbs to one of the most enthusiastic leaders of all times, Thomas A. Edison. If he were alive today, he'd be 147 years old, and I bet he'd *still* be enthusiastic. I want to tell you a story about what happened to him in 1914. He was sixty-seven years old, and at last it seemed that he was on the threshold of his greatest discoveries. Then his factory in West Orange, New Jersey, caught fire one night and was almost completely burned. The damage was terrible, and unfortunately he had insured the buildings and equipment for less than a quarter of their value.

As he stood watching the colossal blaze, his twenty-four-year-old son ran up to him, sure that he would be on the verge of emotional collapse from the magnitude of the disaster. Instead, Thomas was grinning from ear to ear. He shouted: "Where's your mother? Find her. Bring her here. She'll never see anything like this as long as she lives."

The next morning, examining the ruins, Edison told his son, "There's great value in disaster. All our mistakes are burned up. Thank God we can start anew." And three weeks later, Edison produced the world's first phonograph. His buildings were destroyed but he was not.[2]

Now, that's enthusiasm! I suppose there's such a thing as being *too* enthusiastic. I read a very astute saying: "If everything is coming your way, you're probably in the wrong lane."[3] But in general, I think most of us suffer from being not enthusiastic enough, rather than too enthusiastic.

Let me tell you another story. My husband was called to be president of the Japan Okinawa Mission in 1968, so he had responsibility for the LDS Pavilion at the 1970 World's Fair in Osaka. The space we were assigned was with the Japanese exhibits in the domestic area, not the international area. Some people were disturbed by this, but I think it was an inspired choice. If we had been in the international exhibit, our modest pavilion would have been dwarfed by those gigantic exhibits from the United States and the Soviet Union and other world powers.

My husband, Ed, thought it was just right. He told the

missionaries and members: "We're right where the Lord wants us. Everybody has to pass us on the way to the Japanese exhibit and everybody has to pass us on the way to the rest rooms. We're going to get a lot of traffic. On one side of us is the Takara cosmetics exhibit and on the other is the Kodak exhibit. So they'll go to the Takara and get beautiful on the outside, then they'll come to us and get beautiful on the inside, and then they'll go next door and get their picture taken!"

Well, from the time the exhibit opened in the morning until the time it closed late at night, the Japanese people walked through four abreast in a steady stream, looking at the display on the purpose of life and listening to the missionaries. And when the Crown Prince came to visit the exposition, our pavilion was one of four or five that he insisted on seeing. Enthusiasm pays!

Be Appreciative

The third characteristic on my personal leadership list is to be appreciative of others. Appreciate their efforts. Appreciate who they are. Appreciate being in the same world with them. I'd like to tell you a story about President Spencer W. Kimball, who was the most appreciative person I have ever known. When Ed was a Regional Representative, we attended an area conference in Japan. Our second son, Bob, had just completed his mission in Nagoya, and we were able to pick him up and take him with us to this conference.

Bob was still wearing his name tag; when President Kimball saw him, he shook hands with him, then drew him down and kissed him on the cheek and embraced him, saying, "Thank you for serving an honorable mission. Thank you for bearing your testimony to these wonderful people." Bob was overcome with this sense of appreciation and love from the prophet.

Every morning when the whole party would get on the bus to drive to the enormous Olympics building, President Kimball was the last one on the bus. He had been out in the parking lot being sure that everyone else got on. And when he took his seat, he was there for only a minute before he was walking up and down the aisle, shaking hands with everyone, asking how they'd slept, asking if they were comfortable. He was tending his flock, walking the earth as the Savior did. The appreciation he showed had a tremendous influence on people.

Enjoy Change

You can tell that I'm really into enjoyment, because my fourth point is also about enjoyment. As leaders, we should enjoy change. Sometimes that's a hard thing to do, especially if we've made a mistake that's embarrassing to us or if we've committed a sin of which we need to repent. It's also hard if circumstances impose a change on you that you don't want—for instance, developing an illness that makes all your hair fall out. Change looks painful and unpleasant under these circumstances.

Well, if you haven't learned already that change is inevitable, I'm sure it's only a matter of days before reality catches up with you. So find ways to enjoy the process of change. I was interested to read in an article about how army officers are trained at West Point that change is very much involved in the skills they learn. It pointed out that making mistakes was part of the learning process, and that cadets had to be allowed to make their own decisions, right or wrong. And evaluation is a continual part of the process: evaluation by oneself, evaluations by superiors, ratings by peers, and even evaluations by subordinates. Cadets learn to seek responsibility and to take responsibility for their actions. Cadets aren't supposed to wait for others to tell them how to solve a problem, and they're never supposed to say, "It's not my job." Because mistakes are inevitable, a mistake is not a big deal. How they *handle* the mistake is important. And what's the right way? Admit errors, accept criticism, and promptly correct the matter.

Think of other wonderful names for change: hope, repentance, achievement, problem-solving, creativity. What if we could see our potential as the Lord sees it? What if we knew our strengths and talents as clearly as he does? Learn from your mistakes and relish your power to change.

Be Kigatsuku

The fifth point in my personal list of leadership characteristics is to be *kigatsuku*. You may already know that *kigatsuku* is one of my favorite Japanese words—it means an inner desire to do something good without being told. When you see a need, do what you can to meet that need. It's okay if no one else has seen that need, and it's okay if thousands of people don't immediately jump on your bandwagon. If you and I thought exactly alike, one of us would not be necessary. But the world needs each one of us—our separate gifts, our separate creativities, our separate perceptions.

At a BYU women's conference some years ago, I was thrilled by Cécile Pelous, a former Relief Society president and fashion designer from Paris who spends every penny she can save or raise and three months of each year in India, serving the poor. She's definitely a *kigatsuku* person. When she sees a need, she doesn't just tell someone else about it. She personally does something.

She was once asked, "Why are you in India doing all of that on your own? Don't you know the Church is supposed to do that?"

Her reply: *"This* is the Church. *Me.* I'm a member of this Church, and this is the Church doing this."

As a former Relief Society president, she speaks of how frustrated she would get when ward members expressed a desire to serve but did nothing. She says, "Too often it seemed like I had to take their hands and put their fingers on the right buttons and say, 'Now push. Now do it.' Everything had to be done under some direction of the Church. We just don't see the opportunities all around us to serve and to help."

For some, she says, the Church becomes a blinder, preventing them from seeing the whole picture. "Yet really the Church is there to remove any blinders we might have. It's not there to tell us we can't have friends outside the Church or to prohibit us from getting involved in non-LDS sponsored projects."[4]

I recently learned about a creative young woman, Donna Fritz-Bearden, who is known as the "Underwear Lady of Wake County." When she was a student volunteer, the soup kitchen coordinator mentioned that it was fairly easy to get clothing for the needy but nobody ever donated underwear. Donna was a student at Columbia Union College in Maryland, and she immediately headed a campus "Drop Your Drawers" drive with large boxes all over campus. The students loved it. The first year, they bought and donated 700 pieces of "new underpants, T-shirts, thermal underwear, socks, hats, slips, bras, even pantyhose." The next year, they donated about twice that many. When she graduated, she became director of communications for Family Services in Wake County, North Carolina, and launched an annual drive that now collects more than 4,000 pieces of underwear a year.[5]

Now, these two examples are sort of public. They involve groups of people, and at least part of Cécile's and Donna's success depends on telling the story of their projects so that they can attract more support. There is nothing wrong with that, but I want to add a caution. Sometimes we let our lights shine in good deeds, and then we run around with mirrors flashing beams of light into everybody else's eyes. True leadership rests firmly on a solid foundation of good deeds that don't have to be known to anyone. This is a lesson that Elder William R. Bradford taught beautifully:

> The young people of a certain ward had worked to earn the large sum of money needed to go on an adventure trip. I had had some acquaintance with their bishop. He called and asked if I would help him get some news publicity so that these young people would be recognized for the fine things they were doing.
>
> I said that I would not help him. He was surprised and asked why. I answered that although it was commendable that the young people had worked hard to earn this money, some

184

things are interesting while other things are important, and that there might be a higher purpose for the funds they had obtained.

I explained that my ministry takes me into countries where the people are less privileged than where he lives. I explained that the amount of money these fine young people had earned would keep several missionaries from these areas in the field for their entire missions.

He said, "Are you asking me to have these young people donate their funds to the general missionary fund of the Church?"

I said, "No, I have not asked you to do that. I have just said that there are finer things to do." I explained that I was not against the kind of project they were planning but that there must be a balance, and, by comparison, some things are interesting while other things are important.

Later the bishop said that he had talked to the young people and that they wanted to sacrifice their adventure trip and donate all the money to the general missionary fund. He asked if they could bring the check and have their picture taken with me as they made the donation and if they could have the picture and an article put into the news.

I said no. Then I said, "You might consider helping your young people learn a higher law of recognition. Let them feel the joy and gain the treasure in their heart and soul that come from silent, selfless service." . . .

The reward for doing selfless projects is a nearness to divinity, a worthiness for the companionship of the Spirit.[6]

May I suggest that when you see a need, you consider that your perception is the Spirit's way of giving you a little calling, a little job that comes directly from the Lord, not necessarily from your bishop. Be *kigatsuku*. Say yes to these little callings. Some of them will last only ten minutes; others may last a lifetime.

Create Thrive-Safe Environments

The sixth quality on my personal list of leadership is to build environments where people can thrive in safety, where growth is encouraged. We hear a lot about self-esteem and its importance, and I happen to believe that good leaders *always* increase people's self-esteem. Sometimes they can do it directly. Enthusiasm and appreciation are two invaluable direct tools. But if praise is insincere, or if people are complimented for something they *know* they didn't do well, then self-esteem actually dwindles. Sometimes self-esteem has to accompany change, repentance, and growth in competence. In cases like these, the most important thing we can do is to help create safe places for growth—thrive-safe environments, I call them.

I was interested in an article about an organizational effectiveness consultant who was asked to conduct a family camp for the people of her church. She said:

> Over and over again, as I have worked with people in the church who had good self-esteem, I have noticed they are able to grow, change, and resolve difficulties. Those who flounder seem to lack the feeling that they are unique, that they have value. Not only does this seem to be valid for individuals, but it's also true for groups and congregations. . . .
>
> [We] identified behaviors needed in our stake congregations to promote healthy self-esteem. These included listening attentively, creating a safe environment for all ages, using nonverbal acceptance, trusting, respecting all opinions, accepting diversity, being open and honest but kind, risking, reconciling, forgiving, esteeming, validating, celebrating all ages, and being genuine.

These are all skills I know you're aware of, but it's the next part that I want you to pay particular attention to. She continues:

> We discovered that self-esteem cannot be given to anyone. However, individuals and congregations [or apartments or

wards or family home evening groups or student government units] can provide an affirming environment in which people can more realistically choose to esteem themselves and others. . . .

Self-worth is the development of a good personal relationship with God. [One of the participants wrote:] "God calls us to self-esteem because in our accepting who we are and what we are, we accept God's handiwork. We glorify the God who created us when we affirm the worth of the one created. To accept self as a person of worth, unfinished though we may be, is to free God to lead us in the journey of becoming. Self-esteem has to do with an awareness of how much God loves and trusts us. It is in the humble recognition of that love and trust that we gently and patiently touch the lives of those he places in our hands . . . : family members, children, neighbors, other disciples, [and the] stranger at our door."[7]

Now, if we can create safe environments in which people can feel listened to and loved and trusted, then we've created an immensely powerful tool for change in their lives. Because it's indirect, sometimes it seems too complicated, but I want to tell you that it's not. This goes back to enjoying the process and participating in that process with delight and authenticity.

I spent twenty-three years of my career in the classroom, where I could have a personal relationship with each child. Then I spent the next ten years as a principal, where my influence on the children was somewhat indirect, exercised mostly through their teachers. When a parent or a teacher mentioned to me that a child was having trouble, I watched that child the next time I was in the room. I remember one little second-grader named Darren who was having real trouble with number concepts. I watched him closely, and it seemed obvious to me that the problem was the abstractness of the numbers. So when I talked with the teacher after my visit, I suggested, "Have you thought of trying some manipulatives with Darren?"

"Why, no," she said. "Do you think it would work?"

"Maybe," I said. "It does look to me as if we need to do something different with him right now." She was dubious, but she agreed to try number objects that he could touch and move around with his fingers.

The next time I saw her, she had a big grin. "Darren got it!" she exclaimed.

I just smiled and said, "Great!"

Now, as a principal, my job was to exercise leadership, but I didn't do it by replacing the teacher. And I didn't bring in a handbook of "One Hundred and Thirteen Rules for Teaching Math to Second-Graders" and inundate her with directions. Instead, I looked at Darren and his problem with learning his numbers. I looked at my teacher and saw her problem with not seeing what Darren's problem was. I checked my own experience about a solution that seemed to make sense, and I made a suggestion. Then I stepped out of the way and let her have the experience of success. She could do it because she was in a safe environment where she knew she was trusted and appreciated.

Conclusion

We've examined several ideas about what makes an effective leader, but the most important leadership quality that any of us can have is to develop a close, warm relationship with the Savior—to feel in ourselves the love that he feels for us, the love that he wants us to share with others. We often talk about the Atonement in universal terms. "Christ died for all of us," we say. Well, that's not the way I feel about it. I know that Christ died not just for all of us in a group, but for *each* of us. He died for you. He died for me. That's how much he loves you. That's how much he loves me. Remember that. He didn't just die for all of us, he died for each of us.

We are incomplete, imperfect, and limited in our understandings and abilities. It is the grace of God that makes us whole and perfects us. People didn't think Christ was beautiful or perfect when he walked among them, either. He looked human. He acted human. Out of the human bits and pieces of his life, out of the dustiness and the hunger and thirst, out of the misunderstandings and the limitations, he brought a fulness of grace and truth. Into a world of sorrow, he brought a fulness of joy. Into a world of suspicion and mistrust, he brought perfect love.

I bear you my testimony that he is the only leader we can follow in perfect confidence, in utter trust, in total love. Let me tell you the story of a convert in the early days of the Church. His name was John Murdock. In Kirtland, his wife died giving birth to twins, just at the time that the newborn twins of Joseph and Emma Smith died at birth. He gave his children to Joseph and Emma to comfort them in their loss, and they were raised as the Smiths' children, though the baby boy died of pneumonia that he caught when a mob broke into the house and dragged Joseph Smith outside. The minutes of the School of the Prophets record a vision that was granted to John Murdock, this faithful and self-sacrificing convert. The members of the School were instructed by Joseph Smith, with the promise that those who were pure in heart would see a heavenly vision. John Murdock believed what he was taught and acted on it. He records this experience:

> About midday the visions of my mind were opened and the eyes of my understanding were enlightened, and I saw the form of a man, most lovely. The visage of his face was round and fair as the sun, his hair a bright silver gray, curled in most majestic form; his eyes a keen, penetrating blue, and the skin of his neck a most beautiful white. He was covered from the neck to the feet with a loose garment of pure white—whiter than any garment I had ever before seen. His countenance was most penetrating, and yet most lovely.

All these details, I believe, convince us that John Murdock really saw someone. He was not confused or dazzled to the point that he could not observe. But what is truly important to me is the

189

effect on John Murdock of this vision. He says: "When the vision was closed up, it left to my mind the impression of love, for months, and I never before felt it to that degree."[8]

Think of the sweetness of that "impression of love," an impression that lasted keenly and sweetly for many months and lingered on John Murdock's soul. This is not a blessing to John Murdock only. It's a promise to all of us. The scriptures promise us:

> It shall come to pass that every soul who forsaketh his sins and cometh unto me, and calleth on my name, and obeyeth my voice, and keepeth my commandments, shall see my face and know that I am;
>
> And that I am the true light that lighteth every [one] that cometh into the world. (D&C 93:1–2)

The light of Christ shines on you and on me. It shines on each needy brother and sister whose hunger for spiritual truths is as great as his or her hunger for bread. That's why we're here on earth—because of our love for Christ that enabled us to choose his side in the war in heaven. That's what will bring us home—the love of Christ that did not turn back even at the brink of death. That's why we can reach out to others—because of his love that we can share, love that is bountiful and joyous and inexhaustible and that will lead us as we help lead others back home.

BASKETS AND BOTTLES

I love Paul's statement: "There is neither Jew nor Greek, there is neither bond nor free, there is neither male nor female: for ye are all one in Christ Jesus" (Galatians 3:28). I thought of this scripture when the number of Latter-day Saints outside the United States edged ever so slightly past the number of Church members inside the United States. That slight shift is an important reminder of the international nature of the Church. Paul's Jews did not stop being Jews, nor did the bondpersons become free, but their larger identity as Christians was more important than these other identities. So it is with us in the Church. We too are "all one in Christ Jesus."

The relationship of the international church and the North American church has entered my mind as I have participated in leadership training in such places as the Philippines, New Zealand, Australia, Tonga, Fiji, Mexico, Honduras, Guatemala, Samoa, Korea, and Japan. In all these places we participated in two, sometimes three meetings a day with wonderful, faithful Saints, and traveled in between. We worked hard and long. People said, "Oh, you must be so tired." On the contrary, we had a feeling of being borne up "as on eagles' wings" (D&C 124:18), because we were renewed by the love and unity of our sisters and brothers. We have seen the daughters of Zion "awake, and arise . . . and put on [their] beautiful garments" (Moroni 10:31) in response to the good news of the gospel. We have taught, but—and this is the point I want to stress—we have also learned.

I want to invite all of us to consider what it means that The Church of Jesus Christ of Latter-day Saints has taken this step into greater internationalization. Everyone knows that the North American church has given missionaries and money and manuals for many years to the international church. Now it is time to ask, what gifts can the international church give to the larger church? What lessons can be learned from the international church? I think we are just beginning to explore what these questions could mean.

Perhaps the most important lesson is what constitutes the core principles of the gospel, as opposed to cultural packaging. The principles are essential, but the packaging is optional. Let me give you a simple example. Picture a bottle of Utah peaches, prepared by a Utah homemaker to feed her family during a snowy season. Hawaii homemakers don't bottle fruit. They pick enough for a few days and store it in baskets. Mangoes, bananas, pineapples, and papayas might be picked by a Polynesian homemaker to feed her family in a climate where fruit ripens all year round.

The basket and the bottle are different containers, but the content is the same: food for a family. Is the bottle right and the basket wrong? No, they are both right. They are forms appropriate to the culture and the needs of the people. And they are both appropriate for the content they carry.

The forms could be very different—a woven cloth bag, a backpack, a cardboard box, a cookie tin with a tight-fitting lid, a pottery jug, or a self-sealing plastic container. As long as it qualifies as a suitable container for the family's food, it is appropriate.

Now let me apply this example to my question about the contributions of the international church to the larger church. Our unity grows from what we have in common all around the world. Those principles are the doctrines and ordinances of the gospel, our faith in the Savior, our testimonies of the scriptures, our gratitude for guidance from living prophets, and our sense of ourselves as a people striving to be Saints. These are the principles of the gospel. These are the contents of the basket and the bottle. But there are many different ways we can present and understand and apply these principles.

I would like to suggest three things: First, let us be sensitive to the unchanging and powerful core principles of the gospel. Let us understand that they matter most. Let us build firm foundations on these principles. Then when the rains fall and the floods come, our house will be "founded upon a rock" and it will not fall (Matthew 7:25).

Second, let us seek with delight to learn how those principles work themselves out in different cultures, generations, and fellow-citizens of the Saints who are in lands distant from ours. Let us, worldwide, seek to understand and delight in cultural differences.

Third, let us humbly and with consecration offer the gifts with which we individually have been blessed. I hope we will each increase the welcome in our hearts for those of cultural and ethnic groups that differ from those in which we were raised. But I also earnestly entreat us to offer and accept gifts within the smaller circles of our families, wards, and communities. Let us do this so we can learn from each other and grow together.

For years now, I have been listening to the women of the Church. I have learned from all of them. I have learned from divorced mothers who are struggling to raise their children alone. I have learned from women who long to be married but are not, from women who yearn for children but cannot bear them, from women who are at risk from emotional and physical abuse in their homes. I have learned from women who work in their homes and women who work outside their homes. I have learned from women who endure chemical dependencies, memories of childhood sexual abuse, and chronic illness.

Not many of these women thought they were giving me a gift.

Most of them thought they were asking for help. But all of them blessed me and enriched me by their willingness to share.

Most of us willingly share gifts of music, poetry, gospel insights, and even hilarious family doings. But I want particularly to mention those who feel that their troubles and problems mean that they have little to give. To such, both men and women, I feel to say: Please offer on the altar of consecration the experiences that have hurt you as well as the experiences that have helped you. You have much to teach the Church. And the Church has much to learn from you.

I have been blessed all my life, both by the international church and by the North American church. I grew up in Hawaii when it was not yet a state. My parents are Japanese. My languages were Japanese at home, English at school, and pidgin with my friends. When I was called to the Relief Society general presidency, President Gordon B. Hinckley counseled me: "You bring a peculiar quality to this presidency. You will be recognized as one who represents those beyond the borders of the United States and Canada and, as it were, an outreach across the world to members of the Church in many, many lands. They will see in you a representation of their oneness with the Church." He gave me a blessing that my tongue might be loosed as I spoke to the people.

I do not speak Korean or Spanish or Tongan. But when I received my assignment to go among the Relief Society sisters and their priesthood leaders where those languages were spoken, I was filled with a great desire to speak to them in their own language. I drew strength from President Hinckley's words of comfort and blessing. With the help of the Church translation department and good coaches who spent hours working with me, I was blessed to deliver my addresses in Spanish, Korean, and Tongan as I went among those people. I could feel the Spirit carrying my words to their hearts, and I could feel the Spirit bringing back to me their love and their faith, to uphold me in my responsibilities.

Whether our gifts are peaches or papaya, and whether we

bring them in bottles or baskets, I pray that we will offer them to each other in charity and consecration, becoming spiritually involved one with another. I pray that we will also open our hearts that we may receive the gifts of others in humility and thanksgiving, knowing that we are all one in Christ Jesus. Father in Heaven, may we be one and may we be thine (see D&C 38:27).

NOTES

Chapter 1
Sanctuary

1. Larry Barkdull, "Cameo: An Anchor to Latter-day Women," *Cameo: Latter-day Women in Profile*, November 1993, 4–6.

2. Thomas S. Monson, "Hallmarks of a Happy Home," *Ensign*, November 1988, 69, 71.

3. As summarized in "Follow the Lord's Blueprint for Strong Homes, Families Urged," *Ensign*, March 1985, 83.

4. James E. Faust, "Where Is the Church?" *Ensign*, August 1990, 64–66.

Chapter 2
Trust in the Lord

1. Ezra Taft Benson, "The Single Adult Sisters of the Church," address at the General Women's Meeting, 24 September 1988, reprinted as pamphlet, 3, 6, 7, 8.

2. As quoted in "Priesthood Brethren Asked to Be Christ's Servants," *Ensign*, July 1993, 75.

3. Judith Stewart Corey, "Living Through Divorce," *Signs of the Times*, October 1992, 8–9.

4. "To Everything There Is a Season," October 12, 1993, devotional at the Marriott Center.

5. "All in a Day's Work," *Reader's Digest*, January 1992, 119.

Chapter 3
Doors and Thresholds

1. José Luis González-Galado and Janet N. Playfoot, *My Life for the Poor: Mother Teresa of Calcutta* (San Francisco: Harper & Row, 1985), 10.

2. Item in "Update," *Signs of the Times,* October 1992, 6.

3. Cherill Warnock, Letter to Chieko N. Okazaki, October 5, 1992.

4. In Malcolm Muggeridge, *Something Beautiful for God: Mother Teresa of Calcutta* (New York: Walker and Company/Phoenix Press, 1971; large print edition 1984), 119–21.

5. LaRene Gaunt, "One Voice," *Ensign,* April 1993, 46.

Chapter 4
Coins: Lost, Caesar's, and Christ's

1. Loren Seibold, "The Imprint on the Coin: A Meditation for Tax Times," *Signs of the Times,* April 1993, 27.

Chapter 5
Free to Choose

1. *Conference Report,* April 1950, 32.

2. M. Russell Ballard, "Gordon B. Hinckley: An Anchor of Faith," *Ensign,* September 1994, 10.

3. As quoted in *A Thought for Today,* edited by Theron C. Liddle (Salt Lake City: Deseret News Press, 1961, 31.

4. Henrik Als, "Danish Basketball Star and Future Missionary Vows, 'Never on Sunday,'" *Church News,* 14 August 1993, 7.

5. Eleanor Knowles, *Howard W. Hunter* (Salt Lake City: Deseret Book, 1994), 282.

6. Statement at press conference, 6 June 1994, photocopy in my possession.

7. Howard W. Hunter, "The Temple of Nauvoo," *Ensign,* September 1994, 62–63.

8. As quoted in Jeffrey R. Holland, "President Thomas S. Monson: Finishing the Course, Keeping the Faith," *Ensign,* September 1994, 12.

9. Launie Severinsen, "Alternative," 27 February 1992, typescript in my possession.

10. As quoted in *Golden Words of Faith, Hope, and Love,* edited by Louise Bachelder (Mount Vernon, Virginia: Peter Pauper Press, 1969), 51.

11. Jeffrey R. Holland, "President Thomas S. Monson: Finishing the Course, Keeping the Faith," *Ensign,* September 1994, 12–13.

12. As quoted in Editors of Canari Press, *Random Acts of Kindness* (Berkeley, California: Canari Press, 1993), 120.

13. Ibid., 121.

Chapter 6
A Disciple's Heart

1. Maxwell Anderson, *Joan of Lorraine: A Play in Two Acts* (Washington, D.C.: Anderson House, 1947), 127.

2. Ezra Taft Benson, "Jesus Christ, Our Savior and Redeemer," *Ensign*, June 1990, 2.

3. Jose Luis Gonzalez-Galado and Janet N. Playfoot, *My Life for the Poor: Mother Teresa of Calcutta* (San Francisco: Harper & Row, Publishers, 1985), 31.

4. Lowell Thomas, "The Day the Sun Went Out," in *A New Treasury of Words to Live by*, edited by William Nichols (New York: Simon and Schuster, 1957), 59–60.

Chapter 7
Simple Human Kindness

1. Quoted in Malcolm Muggeridge, *Something Beautiful for God: Mother Teresa of Calcutta* (New York: Walker and Company/Phoenix Press, 1971; large print edition 1984), 96.

2. Eric Marshall and Stuart Hample, comps. *Children's Letters to God*, enl. ed. (New York: Pocket Books, 1975), not paginated.

3. John H. Sisley, Jr., untitled anecdote in *The Prince of Peace Is Born* (pamphlet) (Carmel, NY: Guideposts Associates, 1991), not paginated.

4. Harold Wolfgramm, "Three-Minute Profile: Grandma Mary," *This People*, vol. 12, no. 4 (December 1991):77–78.

5. Dalai Lama, as quoted in Editors of Canari Press, *Random Acts of Kindness* (Berkeley, CA: Conari Press, 1993), 20.

6. Suzy Becker, *The All Better Book* (New York: Workman Publishing, 1992), not paginated.

7. Wilma Hepker, "Survival Tactics for Volunteers" *Signs of the Times*, October 1993, 13.

8. Pat Christian, "Santa Gets a Hand from 88-year-old Henrie," Provo, Utah, *Daily Herald*, 26 October 1993, B-1. Born in Fairview in 1905, she moved to Provo in 1923 when she was 16. She graduated from BYU in 1931 and taught English and sewing to students in Colonia Juarez Mexico for two years before returning to Utah and meeting her husband-to-be. They were married in the Manti LDS Temple in 1933.

9. As quoted in Editors of Canari Press, *Random Acts of Kindness* (Berkeley, California: Conaria Press, 1993), 50.

10. Jay M. Todd, "President Howard W. Hunter, Fourteenth President of the Church," *Ensign*, July 1994, 4–5.

Chapter 9
Who We Are, Whose We Are

1. Patricia Sheranian, "Amelia Smith McConkie: A Life of Preparation and Service," *Cameo: Latter-day Women in Profile*, November 1993, 15–16.

Chapter 10
Lifelong Learning and Literacy

1. "Church Efforts to Improve Literacy," interview with Elaine L. Jack, Relief Society general president, *Ensign*, October 1993, 79.

2. As quoted in *Great Quotes from Great Teachers* (Glendale Heights, IL: Great Quotations Publishing Company, 1994), 28.

3. R. Val Johnson: South Africa: Land of Good Hope," *Ensign*, February 1993, 34–35, 37–38.

4. Jana Seiter, Letter to Church Literacy Program: "Dear Sisters," March 12, 1994.

5. Carrie P. Jenkins, "Tough Medicine for Tough Times," *Brigham Young Magazine*, February 1993, 27.

Chapter 11
Thanksgiving: To Hold in Remembrance

1. Elaine A. Cannon, "Preparing to Make a Difference," *Brigham Young University 1981–82 Fireside and Devotional Speeches* (Provo, Utah: University Publications, 1982), 48.

2. Eric Marshall and Stuart Hample, comps., *Children's Letters to God*, enl. ed. (New York: Pocket Books, 1975), not paginated.

3. Julie A. Dockstader, "A Blessing All My Life," *Church News*, 4 April 1992, 16.

4. Donald McCullough, "Insight," *Time With God; New Century Version* (Dallas: Word Bibles, 1991), 593.

5. Fran Vetter, "Go Back Home, Now!" *Ensign*, January 1993, 71.

Chapter 12
Christmas Extravagance

1. Commentary accompanying "'Twas in the Moon of Wintertime," Pamela Conn Beall and Susan Hagen Nipp, *Wee Sing for Christmas* (Los Angeles: Price/Stern/Sloan, 1985), 24–25.

2. As quoted in Lynn Arave, "Keep True Holiday Spirit, LDS Leaders Counsel," *Deseret News*, 5–6 December 1994, B-1.

Chapter 13
"Nothing Shall Be Impossible"

1. Dallin H. Oaks, "Our Strengths Can Become Our Downfall," *BYU Today*, November 1992, 34–38, 42–43.

Chapter 15
Hubs and Spokes: Some Thoughts on Wheels

1. James M. Paramore, "'By the Power of His Word Did They Cause Prisons to Tumble,'" *Ensign*, November 1992, 10.

2. Ibid.

3. Annie L. Peachey, "The Vegetable Garden," photocopy in my possession.

4. Spencer W. Kimball, Salt Lake Institute of Religion Devotional, October 22, 1976, 2.

5. Charlene Renberg Winters, "Despite Obstacles, Nursing Dean Achieves Childhood Dream," *BYU Today*, November 1992, 12–13.

6. Typescript of interview in my possession.

Chapter 16
Lives Woven Together

1. *What is a Mother: Children's Responses*, Lee Parr McGrath and Joan Scobey, comps. (New York; Simon & Schuster, 1968), not paginated.

2. Annette Paxman Bowen, "Words a Mother Longs to Hear," *Ensign*, June 1992, 66–67.

3. B. W. Cook, "Heloise's Hints Are a Family Tradition," *Newport Beach/Costa Mesa Daily Pilot*, September 4, 1993, A-8 and A-9.

4. "Women's Voices" manuscript, 12 April 1991, photocopy of typescript in my possession.

Chapter 17
Six Pleasures of Leadership

1. Gil Dorland and John Dorland, "Character Building," *Sky*, July 1993, 29.

2. Victoro M. Parachin, "Making the Most of Failure," *Signs of the Times*, April 1993, 8–9.

3. Harvey Egan, in "Update," *Signs of the Times*, February 1933, 6.

4. Carrie P. Jenkins, "Cécile Pelous: Rubbing Away the Hurt," *BYU Today*, July 1992, 27.

5. Jeannette Johnson, "The Underwear Lady of Wake County," *Signs of the Times*, May 1992, 19.

6. "Selfless Service," *Friend,* September 1992, inside front cover; adapted from general conference address, *Ensign,* November 1987, 75–76.

7. Mary A. Kellog, "A Reunion Experiment," *Saints Herald,* August 1992, 12–14.

8. John Murdock, as quoted in Blaine M. Yorgason, "The Prophet Joseph's Grand Design," *Latter-day Digest,* vol. 2, no. 4, August 1993, 68.

SOURCES

Chapter 1, "Sanctuary," was adapted from addresses presented at a meeting of the Brigham Young University faculty wives, 15 January 1994, and at a Relief Society regional conference, Cincinnatti, Ohio, 30 May 1995.

Chapter 2, "Trust in the Lord," was adapted from an address presented at a Relief Society regional conference, Placentia, California, 16 October 1993.

Chapter 3, "Doors and Thresholds," was adapted from addresses presented at a devotional for Temple Square missionaries, Salt Lake City, 22 September 1993, and at a Relief Society regional conference, Cleveland, Ohio, 31 May 1995.

Chapter 4, "Coins: Lost, Caesar's, and Christ's," was adapted from addresses presented at a singles fireside, Gilbert, Arizona, 3 December 1993; at a regional conference, Boise, Idaho, 13 March 1994; and at a Relief Society regional conference, Harrisburg, Pennsylvania, 2 June 1995.

Chapter 5, "Free to Choose," was adapted from addresses presented at the Wilford Stake, Salt Lake City, 20 September 1994; at the fall symposium of Collegium Aesculapium, Turtle Bay, Laie, 6 November 1994; and at a sacrament meeting in the Philadelphia Pennsylvania Second Ward, 12 November 1994.

Chapter 6, "A Disciple's Heart," was adapted from addresses presented at a Relief Society conference, Gilbert Ward, Gilbert, Arizona, 3 December 1993, and at a Relief Society meeting, New York City, 30 October 1993.

Chapter 7, "Simple Human Kindness," was adapted from addresses presented at a devotional for Seventies' secretaries, Salt Lake City, 8 August 1993, and at a Young Women standards night, Sandy, Utah, 3 November 1993.

Chapter 8, "Raised in Hope," was adapted from an address presented at the General Relief Society Meeting, 28 September 1996.

Chapter 9, "Who We Are, Whose We Are," was adapted from an address presented at a devotional at the Weber State Institute of Religion, Ogden, Utah, 30 November 1993.

Chapter 10, "Lifelong Learning and Literacy," was adapted from an address presented at a Relief Society regional conference, Blackfoot, Idaho, 29 April 1995.

Chapter 11, "Thanksgiving: To Hold in Remembrance," was adapted from addresses presented at a sacrament meeting, Auwaiolimu Ward, Honolulu, Hawaii, 14 November 1993, and at a regional singles fireside, Victorville, California, 18 September 1994.

Chapter 12, "Christmas Extravagance," was adapted from an address presented to a group in Salt Lake City hosted by Bill and Donna Smart, 9 December 1994.

Chapter 13, " 'Nothing Shall Be Impossible,' " was adapted from an address presented at a regional women's conference, Nashville, Tennessee, 7–8 January 1994.

Chapter 14, "Walking through the Valley of the Shadow," was adapted from addresses presented at a Relief Society regional conference, Farmington, New Mexico, 18 June 1994; at the funeral of Yoshie Viona Okazaki, Kahului, Hawaii, 29 June 1994; and at the funeral of Ken Biesinger, Salt Lake City, 15 September 1994.

Chapter 15, "Hubs and Spokes: Some Thoughts on Wheels," was adapted from an address presented at a meeting of the Wasatch 5th, 6th, and 7th Wards, Salt Lake City, 8 September 1993.

Chapter 16, "Lives Woven Together," was adapted from an address presented at a meeting of the Wasatch Stake Relief Society, Salt Lake City, 12 October 1993.

Chapter 17, "Six Pleasures of Leadership," was adapted from an address presented at the Wright Leadership Seminar, Brigham Young University, 27 January 1994.

Chapter 18, "Baskets and Bottles," was adapted from an address presented at general conference, 6 April 1996.

INDEX

not being made senior
companion, 45–47; greeted
emotionally by mission
president, 48; returning to jobless
situation, 50–52; receiving thanks
from converts years later, 117;
Protestants slipping
anonymously off boat, 118–19
Missionary work, 35
Mistakes: inevitability of, 59, 153–54;
learning from, 182–83
Moffat, Craig, 7
Monson, Thomas S., 4–5, 63–65
Mordecai, uncle of Esther, 68–69
Mortality: trials inherent in, 16–17;
physical requirements of, 50, 52;
mistakes as part of, 59, 153–54;
requires choices, 67; as valley of
shadow, 148; we accepted
conditions of, in premortal
council, 154; as probationary
state, 155; varying circumstances
of, 160
Mother Teresa: gives all her money
away, 34; on person-to-person
service, 38; on "spoiling" poor, 73;
on being unwanted, 75–76
Motherhood, 169–71
Murdock, John, 189–90
Music, sharing gifts of, 131–33

Names, importance of, 96–97, 175–76
Nazi soldier, kindness shown by,
82–83
Needs: emotional versus physical, 7;
learning to recognize, 110; filling,
without waiting for assignment,
183–85
Newkirk, Gladys, 108–9, 166–67
Nurse, woman overcomes handicaps
to become, 164–65

Oaks, Dallin H., 142
Okazaki, Andrew, 15–16, 93–94, 97,
106
Okazaki, Bob, 15–16, 79–80, 93, 106,
162–63, 181

Okazaki, Chris, 15–16, 93–94, 97–98,
106
Okazaki, Ed: death of, 1, 8–9, 84–85,
152, 156; instructs missionary to
end fast, 7; love of, for bishop,
10–11; writes to missionary
regarding senior-companion
status, 45–46; love of, for
missionaries, 48; asks, "What
would Jesus do?" 80; appreciative
attitude of, 118; champions wife
for school superintendent,
143–44; buys tandem bike, 163;
oversees LDS pavilion at World's
Fair, 180–81
Okazaki, Gordon, 83–84
Okazaki, Ken, 79–80, 162–63
Okazaki, Matthew, 15–16, 93, 102–3,
106
Okazaki, Viona, 83–85
Otake, Fumiko, 174

Painting hung in temple, 2–3
Pansy grows out around brick, 88
Parable of lost coin, 42–43
Paramore, James, 160–61
Patience, 24, 75
Peace: sources of, 2; of temple, 62
Pelous, Cecile, 183–84
Perry, L. Tom, 5, 23, 24
Peter, 17, 30–33
Potential, eternal, 163–64
Prayer: power of, in lives of friends,
7–8; honesty in, 18–19, 146;
failing to recognize answers to,
33–34; as hinge, 36; of
discouraged missionary, 36–37;
for self-acceptance, 45; as
limitless conversation, 73;
sharing gift of, 133–34; personal,
145–46
Premortal existence, 152–54, 175
Principal of inner-city high school,
story of, 112–14
Priorities, 25, 73
Prison, Peter's escape from, 30–33